How I Sold 1 Million eBooks in 5 Months!

John Locke

The New York Times Best Selling Author
Donovan Creed & Emmett Love Novels

TELEMACHUS
PRESS

DISCLAIMER

This publication is designed to provide general information regarding the subject matter covered. However, rules, regulations, laws, practices and the interpretation of same often change or vary from state to state and company to company, particularly with regard to social media, communication, and social media companies. Because each situation is different, the reader is advised to consult with his or her own advisor regarding that individual's specific situation.

Neither the author nor the publisher assume any responsibility for any errors or omissions, nor do they represent or warrant that the information, ideas, plans, actions, suggestions, and methods of operation contained herein is in all cases true, accurate, appropriate, or legal. It is the reader's responsibility to consult with his or her own advisor before putting any of the enclosed information, ideas, or practices into play. The author and the publisher specifically disclaim any liability resulting from the use or application of the information contained in this book, and the information is not intended to serve as legal advice related to individual situations.

This book is a work of the author's experience and opinion. Names, characters, places and incidents are either the product of the author's imagination or are used fictitiously. Any resemblance to actual persons, living or dead, or to actual events or locales is entirely coincidental.

Cover Designed by: Telemachus Press, LLC

Published by: Telemachus Press, LLC
http://www.TelemachusPress.com

Visit the author website: http://www.DonovanCreed.com

ISBN: 978-1-935670-90-2 (eBook)
ISBN: 978-1-935670-91-9 (Paperback)

Printed in the United States of America
10 9 8 7 6 5 4 3 2 1

John Locke

The New York Times Best Selling Author
#1 Best Selling Author on Amazon Kindle

Donovan Creed Series:

Lethal People
Lethal Experiment
Saving Rachel
Now & Then
Wish List
A Girl Like You
Vegas Moon

Emmett Love Series:

Follow the Stone
Don't Poke the Bear!

Acknowledgments

There is not enough room to thank everyone who encouraged me along the way, so I will just mention four: Winslow Eliot, Claudia Jackson, Kate Madison, and Maryruth Barksdale. Winslow, because she was my first Twitter friend, and because she believed in me and eventually wound up editing most of my books. Claudia, because her company, Telemachus Press, publishes all my books and eBooks. I brag on Telemachus so often, there are rumors I own the company or am on the payroll. Not true. I brag on them because they do a great job, and because I appreciate quality, hard work and dedication, and Claudia and her staff never fail to exceed my expectations. Kate, because she is very astute, and has been a wonderful sounding board for this project. Maryruth, because she is my most famous and vocal OOU! The success I've experienced as an author is due in large part to the unwavering, loyal support I receive daily from the world's greatest people: the thousand-plus army of OOU's like Maryruth, who have become my close friends and staunchest supporters. Bless you all, and thank you for being such an important part of my world.

INTRODUCTION

In the space of six months, from September, 2010 to March 2011, John Locke increased his total Kindle *monthly* sales from 63 to 369,115!

He is only the eighth author in the world to have sold 1 million downloads on Kindle, and is the first self-published author in history to have done so!

He is the first self-published author to hit #1 on the Amazon/Kindle Best Seller's List!

He is the first self-published author to hit both #1 and #2 at the same time!

He is a *New York Times* best-selling author!

He has been featured in *The Wall Street Journal* and *Entertainment Weekly*!

He has had:

- *4 of the Top 10 books on Amazon/Kindle at the same time, including #1 and #2!*

- *6 books in the Top 20 at the same time!*

- *7 books in the Top 34 at the same time!*

- *8 books in the Top 50 at the same time!*

Locke's 8th book, *Vegas Moon*, hit #3 on the Best Seller's List just two weeks after its release!

These numbers are not positions within a category. They are positions that include all Kindle sales including fiction, non-fiction, magazine subscriptions, and game apps!

By the middle of March, 2011, it had been calculated that "every 7 seconds, 24 hours a day, a John Locke novel is downloaded somewhere in the world."

In the 5 month period from January 1 to May 31, 2011, John Locke sold more than 1,100,000 eBooks!

...All this was achieved PART TIME, without an agent, publicist, and at virtually no marketing expense.

Now, for the first time ever, John Locke will show you the exact marketing system he created that enabled him to achieve this remarkable success!

Part One

WHEREIN WE DISCUSS . . .

How self-published authors can outsell industry giants.

When, how, and why I publicly announced my arrival on the scene.

Why I held back publication of this book.

My background and credentials.

Some Q&A.

How I spent more than $25,000 discovering what didn't work, and why.

Revenge of the Nerds!

IN HIGH SCHOOL it was jocks vs. nerds. Rich kids vs. others. Beautiful people vs. the rest of us. And they always had the upper hand. We survived it and thought those times were behind us. Then we grew up, wrote books and found ourselves up against the publishing industry, which is like high school on steroids!

I learned early in the game I couldn't compete with the big boys and girls in their arena of hardcover and paperback books. The famous authors have huge corporations backing them, newspaper ads and reviews promoting them, and bookstores displaying them. As a self-published author, I'm boxed out of these marketing opportunities. Worse, I can't afford to offer my print books as cheaply as they can!

I'd like to compete, but it's hard to beat the home team on a playing field that's hopelessly slanted against you!

My character, *Donovan Creed*, has a philosophy of fighting that applies here. He says, *"Never fight your opponent the way he wants to fight you."*

Think about that. For many years self-published authors have been forced to fight in the *traditional* arena, a place where we had almost no chance of *competing*, much less winning. Add to that the *stigma* self-published authors face that no other business on earth imposes. The general public has been conditioned to believe if you're self-published your books don't measure up. And, the media have done all they could to hammer that message home.

The phrase *"vanity publishing"* was almost certainly invented by traditional publishers years ago in order to squash the competition from entrepreneurial authors.

It worked.

By ridiculing and publicly shaming self-published authors for daring to invest in their own talents and abilities, publishing houses were able to elevate themselves to god-like status. What they're saying, when an author believes in his abilities to the extent he's willing to invest his own money to publish a novel, he's writing purely for his vanity!

I have to give credit to the geniuses that came up with this hogwash, because publishing is the only business in the world that has managed to make such a ridiculous notion seem plausible.

When I invested my own money to start my insurance agency no one accused me of making a *vanity* investment. When I invested my own money to buy a life insurance company no one called it a *vanity* investment. When I paid cash for my first office building, planning to lease it out for a profit, no one accused me of making a *vanity* investment. When Bill Gates and Paul Allen invested their time and money into developing code for the Altair computer, no one accused them of writing *vanity* code.

But if Bill Gates and Paul Allen invest their own money to write a book, they're no longer businessmen, they're vain! And any company that charges them to publish that book is catering to their vanity! How absurd is that?

It's laughable. And those who perpetuate the notion are going to be forced to re-think that premise.

Many years ago the publishing industry managed to crush and humiliate men and women who dreamed of writing and selling their books to the public. They created the false impression that the only standard of quality writing is for someone else to invest in your startup in return for a percentage of future profits. You might as well claim I'm less of an investor because I don't ask other people to fund my real estate investments! How is it that self-publishing is the only business where self-funding is considered undignified?

Enter eBooks and ePublishing. eBooks allow a guy like me an opportunity to level the playing field. In fact, eBooks allow me to turn the tables on famous authors and create a situation that is completely unfair to them! Because I can publish an eBook for very little money, I can afford to sell it for 99 cents and still receive a 35 cent profit!

You know what a great gift idea is? A Kindle. An iPad. An eReader. A Nook. These are great gifts because they don't cost a fortune, and they're cool. When your sister or husband gives you a Kindle for your birthday they're saying, "You're smart. You like to read. I'm giving you a thoughtful gift." –And when you receive it, the first thing you want to do is purchase content.

When you look at what's available, you'll find lots of choices, including free books and famous authors, whose titles generally run $9.95 to $14.95. You'll also find John Locke novels for 99 cents. The famous authors' current books are your first choice, of course, so you'll want to get several of those.

But how many can you afford?

After you've downloaded several, and realize you've spent $40 or more, you're still hungry for content, and this is where I come in! You look at a $9.95 book with 138 reviews, 60% positive, and you look at John Locke's 99 cent book with 138 reviews and 80% positive. You see John Locke has nine books available and you calculate you could buy all nine for less than one of the famous author's books!

You think, "I could buy five John Locke novels and a mocha latte for less than *one* famous author's book!" You read the "about the author" section and learn that every book John Locke has written became a best seller, and he is also, in fact, a *New York Times* best-selling author.

You figure, "What the heck. I'll give John a try. I've never heard of him, and he probably sucks, but hey, it's only 99 cents." —And that's the moment I turn the tables on the famous authors, because first, my books may not be great literature, but they certainly don't suck. Second, there's no way in the world the famous authors can afford to price their books for 99 cents, because their publishers would lose a fortune!

As I've been telling people for more than a year, when famous authors are forced to sell their books for $9.95, and I can sell mine for 99 cents, I no longer have to prove my books are as good as theirs. Now the famous authors have to prove their books are *ten times* better than mine! —And in a game like that, I like my chances!

You might say, "Of *course* you're going to do well, John. You've sold more than a million books, received hundreds of positive reviews, and you're a *New York Times* Best Selling author." "Who *couldn't* sell tons of eBooks with that type of resume?"

And I'll respond, "When I started ePublishing one short year ago, I had none of those stats on my resume."

How I got from there...to here...is what the rest of this book is about.

Author Note

How I Sold 1 Million eBooks in 5 Months reveals the marketing system I developed to propel my books to the top of the Amazon/Kindle Best Seller List. I created the system in October, 2010, after having failed miserably for more than a year, trying all the things the "experts" recommended. By October 26th I knew I had created something special, so I posted the following blog to sound the alarm I was coming, and that *Saving Rachel*, an eBook that sold only 16 downloads the month before, was about to take off. Here is that blog, explaining why the traditional publishing world was about to be shaken up.

Thank God for Independent Authors!

Posted <u>October 26, 2010</u> by <u>jplocke</u>

Hang in there, independent authors, because—God love you— you're the future of bookselling! Things are finally changing for self-published authors. Well, maybe not everywhere. Not yet. Certain book stores and publishing houses still look down their noses at us, and maybe some of our snooty friends are still arching a brow and sneering, "So...you're SELF-published?"

Well, don't fault them for it. There will always be those who fail to spot trends. IBM squandered the chance to buy Microsoft for peanuts. Microsoft blew the chance to buy Apple. And Decca Records turned down the Beatles, going so far as to say "The Beatles have no future in show business." Instead, they signed The Tremeloes, who auditioned the same day. (Who?)

But I digress.

It only takes two words to explain why self-published authors are the wave of the future: Electronic Books.

In July, Amazon.com reported eBooks were outselling hard covers nearly two to one! And why not? They're cheaper, they're environmentally friendly, they don't require a trip to the bookstore, you can download them in seconds, free of postage, and you can carry hundreds of them onto an airplane without adding an ounce of weight!

Plain and simple, there has never been a better time in history for the self-published author to compete against the big boys and girls. But before I show you how, let me tell you a quick story: In March, 1963, I was 12 years old, living in Shreveport, Louisiana. Early one Saturday morning, I rode a bus downtown and visited Stan's Record Shop on Texas Street, and bought a brand new record called *Walk Like A Man*, by the Four Seasons. Ever hear of it? I paid ONE DOLLAR for that record, and it was exactly...two minutes and seventeen seconds long. NOW, 47 YEARS LATER, you can download my entire book, *Saving Rachel,* on your Kindle or PC or iPad...for only 99 cents!

Now tell me truly: how can you POSSIBLY beat a deal like that?

Owners of eBook readers are as dedicated a group of readers as can be found anywhere in the world. After having spent hundreds of dollars to acquire their Kindle or Nook or iPad, they're eager to load up their electronic libraries with great books. And never before in history have a major group of book buyers been more willing to take a chance on books written by self-published authors. They can buy an established author's eBook for $10, or they can buy TEN books by ten different independent authors for the same price!

I've received wonderful comments from these ebook buyers. Like how they enjoy "discovering" new talent. In the old days they wouldn't have plunked down $25 for a hardcover or $15 for a paperback written by a self-published author. Now they have a reason to sample our wares, because 99 cents is an afterthought! This group of readers understands something most publishing houses and bookstores have forgotten:

Every best-selling author in the world was at one time—a non-published author!

What I'm saying, Kindle and iPad book buyers will give you a chance! Your books have to be good, of course, because content is king. But if you've got a good product, price is a HUGE factor, and gets your toe in the door.

Bargains are everywhere! Right now, *Saving Rachel* isn't even a blip on the publishing houses' radar. But guess what: it WILL be, because sales are going to start growing like crazy! And there's more: my new books, *Now & Then* and *Wish List* are also available as eBooks! Scroll up a bit and look at the screen to the right of this page and click on the pictures in the VIDEO BAR to watch my book trailers. If you see something that cranks your tractor, you can buy it for 99 cents by clicking on the LINKS to BOOKS section.

—This particular blog was an announcement. I rarely write these. But I knew things were about to change in the eBook arena, and I wanted a chance to be quoted about it. I also wanted to be very obvious that I intended to be a part of the coming revolution. At the time I wrote this blog, I had been offering four eBooks at 99 cents each for eight months and had just brought out a fifth book, *Wish List*. As I said, in September 2010, my biggest selling eBook was *Saving Rachel*, and I sold only 16 copies that month. My record month was seven months earlier, when I sold a whopping 27 copies!

So what changed at the end of October that filled me with such confidence?

I launched my new marketing system the day before posting this announcement!

People are always searching for the silver bullet, the one thing someone else did that can be identified and replicated to ensure success. And although in most cases there is never just one specific event or concept you can point to that changed everything, in my case there was.

That one triggering event occurred on November 3, 2010, and took my books straight to the top of the charts. I knew it would be good, but I had no idea *how* good!

Why I Held Back This Book

I DIDN'T TELL a soul about my discovery for several reasons. Instead, I began writing additional books like crazy. I knew a lot of people were reading my books and if they liked them, I figured they'd want as much product as I could provide. As a marketing guy there's no greater nightmare than whipping a crowd into a buying frenzy and having no product to sell them.

By mid-March, 2011, I had seven out of seven books on the Amazon/Kindle Best Seller List, including spots #1 and #2! By the end of the month I had an eighth book on the list! In May I published a ninth book, and that one also hit the Amazon/Kindle Best Seller list.

You're reading my tenth book now, the book I wrote to help other authors who want to learn what I did to get my books onto the Best Seller List. While there was one triggering event that launched my success, there were a number of supporting elements that had to be in place to maximize the potential of my marketing system. The good news is you're probably utilizing those elements already, and at most you should require only a minor adjustment in your thought process, or refinement in technique or execution in order to be successful.

I'll identify the most original and effective component of my system for you now, so you'll know there is one. I wish I could patent it, but I'll have to settle for copyrighting this book, instead. I call this technique *Loyalty Transfer*.

Try not to jump ahead, because there are several things you should know before we get to that part. But the *Loyalty Transfer* concept alone is worth — okay, don't laugh when I say this — ten thousand bucks! I base that valuation on the amount of money I would have gladly paid for it.

What? I'm giving you a ten thousand dollar idea in a $4.99 eBook, $9.99 paperback?

Yup. And I'm including a wealth of other valuable ideas, too.

And one of the reasons I'm doing that is because I'm the world's biggest jerk.

You see, I could have shared my system seven months ago. I did reference some of these ideas on various blog interviews, but I was always careful not to go into too much detail. And why?

Because I'm a jerk.

Before I developed a sales and marketing system I made tons of mistakes that cost me tons of time and money. How much time? Hundreds and hundreds of hours. How much money? Well over $25,000!

So when I came up with a system that was virtually FREE, what did I do? —Wonderful, caring, thoughtful person that I am?

I kept it to myself.

There are several reasons I didn't share it. For one thing, *I* knew the system worked, but you wouldn't have been impressed, because my sales weren't crazy high yet. So in truth, seven — even four months ago — would have been premature as far as my credibility was concerned. You might not have paid much attention to this book back then. But had I released it even three months ago, you would have been able to benefit.

Another reason I didn't share back then is I know my system works, and didn't want to have to compete against other authors who will not only use it, but might refine it to make it even better. Also, I wanted to hit the million sales mark before sharing it because, well, I'm a little greedy. Also, I wanted to see if the system *itself* worked, so I could be sure my success was not simply due to having written the Donovan Creed series of books (of course, the Donovan Creed series of books had already been out in the world for eight months by October and the world wasn't exactly beating a path!)

Still, I couldn't prove my system was responsible for my success. I mean, most "experts" claimed the only reasons I'd been successful were my 99 cent prices, and the huge holiday spike in sales of Kindle Readers. But if those were the only reasons, why weren't all the other 99 cent authors benefitting from the same holiday spike? That thought was publicly debated, and I sat back and kept my mouth shut while the experts decided it had to be random chance (what?) or the fact people actually liked my books (yay!)

Back in the old days I always thought if I ever wrote a book it would probably be a western. I decided against it after reviewing the Amazon categories and learning that westerns were one of the worst selling genres of books on Kindle! My great idea for a western series remained in my head until I developed this marketing system. At that point I figured if I could get a *western* onto the Amazon/Kindle Best Seller's List, my system would *have* to get credit for being a huge factor in my success.

So I *did* write my western, and used my system to market it, and it *did* hit the Amazon/Kindle Best Seller list...in just two weeks! In the process, I became hooked on the genre, and recently published a sequel that hit the Best Seller List in only seven days!

I may be wrong about this, and if I am, please email me and let me know, and I'll have my friends at Telemachus Press make the correction. But to the best of my knowledge, there have only been two westerns that made the Best Seller list between January and June, 2011. And both of those westerns were written by me. And it's NOT because I'm a great author! Truth is, I'm barely a good one. This is not false modesty, it's the truth, and I'll be the first to say it. By the same token I don't suck as an author, and every now and then something I write may surprise you. I often say, "I *can* write better, I just refuse to!" –And there's a reason for that: I don't write to *impress* my target audience, I write to *entertain* them.

Another reason I held off publishing this book is because I'd been considering offering a series of full-day seminars to teach these concepts in person, at a price that would make it worthwhile to create a bunch of direct competitors. But I eventually decided I didn't want to hit the road again, as I had done for many years when I was much younger.

I could have charged much more for this book. But I don't want to do that, because I sincerely enjoy helping people (eventually!) and if an author is already struggling financially, I'd feel terrible adding to his or her financial burden.

You might say, "If you feel *that* way, offer it for free!"

—Right!

If you invented a system for marketing books that no one else was using, and you knew by revealing it you would create a bunch of direct competitors, don't you feel you should get a couple of bucks to reimburse yourself for the weeks it took to write it all down and have it formatted? At least get your money back for the cover expenses and the uploading to the various eBook formats?

I do.

And if *you* don't invest *something*, even an amount less than five dollars, you certainly aren't going to value the information, and that wouldn't be fair to either of us.

How did I decide on $4.99? In the end I chose this amount for the same reason I decided to sell my novels for 99 cents each — I want you to receive a value you'll consider *crazy* good!

The selling system you're about to read is the exact system I used to sell more than 1,100,000 eBooks in five months. If my system only helps you sell 15 eBooks at 99 cents each, or only *three* eBooks at $2.99, I've made you a profit! But if my system enables you to have a best seller, just imagine how thrilled I'll be to know I helped you achieve something meaningful in your life!

So here it is.

If you skip ahead, your first reaction might be, "It's short!"

There are a lot of people whose perception of value is all screwed up. They feel if I'm charging five bucks there better be at least 320 pages of material. If you're like that, you need to adjust your attitude and think more like a business person. I'm a businessman, and have been all my life. And when you take 300 pages to tell me something that only requires half that, I get very annoyed. I'll pay you four times as much if you can distill your concept into 160 pages I can *use*, because my time is valuable, and I hate filler!

So yeah, it's short. It was short BEFORE I edited forty pages out of the original manuscript, out of respect for your time. I'm not just saying that. I'm a flippin' novelist! You KNOW I could throw in another hundred meaningless pages if I felt you couldn't comprehend the concept that value has nothing to do with excessive wordage. I mean, look at these last two paragraphs, where I've completely wasted your time. Is that what you want?

Look, if you require this book to be twice as long in order to feel you got your money's worth, read it a second time.

So yeah, this is a short book. But it casts a long shadow.

This is not an Ego Book!

THIS BOOK HAS been written for one reason only: to provide a simple system that will enable you to market your book onto the Amazon/Kindle Best Seller's List for virtually no money.

There are no fillers here, no "maybe's." This system is 100% workable. I say "workable" instead of "guaranteed" because I can't guarantee your success. I mean I don't know the quality of your book. If it sucks, it sucks, and all the marketing in the world won't make it a best-seller.

But I can give you this guarantee: however bad your book is, it's better than *Killing Hailey*, which is the worst manuscript ever written. I can say that in all honesty, because I'm the one who wrote it.

OMG that book was bad!

So bad that even the system I'm going to show you couldn't have propelled it past 100 *sales*, let alone onto the top 100! Thankfully, I knew how bad it was, and refused to publish it.

How I Sold... is not an ego book. I mean, sure, I gave you the stats earlier. But I did that in order to establish my credentials. You wouldn't trust my information if it was just a theory, right? But we're past that now, so let's move along.

Well, almost. You'll want my resume, because without it, you might think what I did was a fluke. It wasn't. It was a calculated business idea that began working the minute I quit doing all the things the "experts" told me to do.

I'll make this short: When I was 21 years old, I started selling insurance door to door in Natchitoches, Louisiana. I had no car, no phone, no suit, and no electricity in my apartment. But I created a marketing system that worked. At age 22, I was a State Director. At 23, an Area-Vice President. At 28, a millionaire. By age 35 my net worth exceeded $25 million, and I bought my own life insurance company.

The company I purchased was a shell, meaning it had capital and surplus and 43 state charters, but no agents or employees, and no business on the books. So I designed an insurance product and created a marketing system to recruit agents to sell on straight commission. That year I recruited 6,700 agents! Ten years later, I sold my company at a nice profit, and became a private investor. As of this writing I own sixteen different successful business entities. Two years ago I started writing novels, part time.

Like I said, this isn't an ego book, so let's move along...

First, Some Q & A...

A MAJOR RESERVATION I had about publishing this book is the potential for distractions. I love people, especially authors, but my job as a writer is to write books and build my audience. By writing this book I'm well aware I could receive many emails asking me to mentor you, and help define your target audience, answer your questions, evaluate your books, manuscripts and blogs, and write reviews and blurbs for your novels.

I can't do it!

I love you, and wish you great success, but I just can't. I'm offering you a system I didn't have last year, and hope you'll feel I've done my part by sharing it with you. I'm saving you a fortune in time and money by explaining what didn't work for me, and hope you'll invest the time and energy to figure out how to adapt my system to your specific audience and skill set. I simply can't afford the time commitment required to mentor other authors. Some have asked me to write a paid blog to offer on-going advice, but again, doing so would be a distraction from my writing.

I can already envision your email that starts, "I know you said you don't have time to evaluate other people's blogs, but..."

Onward.

I'd like to address the most common questions I've heard these past few months.

Should I self-publish or hold out for an agent or traditional publisher?

You should self-publish. There's a difference between spending time and investing it. Instead of spending time writing query letters you should invest time writing more novels, or improving the manuscripts you haven't published yet. I never considered traditional publishing because I didn't want to work for someone else. I wanted to write a specific type of book for a specific type of audience, and trusted myself to find that audience. If you know you can find your audience, why pay someone else to do it?

How do I know if my books are good enough?

I can tell you right now your books are probably not very good, or you wouldn't have to ask. But that's okay, because your writing doesn't have to be really good. It just has to be effective.

Haha, I can already hear the abuse I'm going to get for that remark. But if you believe as I do, that writing is a business, you'll see my point.

Example: who writes better, me or Billy Shakespeare? – Shakespeare, of course. But whose book will you take to the beach this summer? –Yeah, that's right, mine! (yes, I'm quite aware Shakespeare wrote plays, not books. Still...)

Quick question: *which is world-class at McDonald's: the food or the business plan?*

The business plan, of course. No one on earth would argue Micky D's food is world class cuisine. It's only good in the context of what it is. McDonald's food is more popular than great. Your grandma's cooking is great. But McDonald's food is more popular. If McDonald's were a book, it would get a *huge* publishing contract. Not because it's great literature, but because it has a proven track record of sales.

With this in mind, should we automatically concede that the classics are better than popular books? What *is* the definition of a great book? Seems to me it's awfully subjective. Some of the worst books I've ever read were considered world-class literature. I wouldn't give you a nickel for most of the books I was forced to read in high school and college. So if you're asking *me* what the definition of a great book is, remember, I'm a businessman. To me, a great book is one that sells. The more it sells, the better it is! Now you can get all high and mighty, or you can go out and sell some books.

Here's my take: your book doesn't have to be world-class. It just has to sell. Don't worry, you'll become a better writer as you go, because you're going to follow my system, and a big part of it is getting feedback from your loyal readers. Their comments will teach you how to be even *more* effective.

Should I take writing courses?

I don't know. I've never taken a writing course or attended seminars because I've always been afraid the more I learn, the less original I'll be. But I'm astonishingly weird, and you should do what works for you. Having said that, if I ever teach a course, you should attend! :-)

This may be a good time for me to ask you something: would you rather be the world's greatest novelist, or the world's best-selling novelist? If it's the latter, perhaps this book can be your starting point.

How much writing experience did you have, John?

I wrote some marketing manuals and a couple of business books thirty years ago, but never tried my hand at writing novels until two years ago. I don't know all the things professionals know, such as how to diagram a novel, or organize a — what's that thing called? —oh yeah, a *plot*. I don't know the proper way to write narrative and dialogue. The books I write only require me to write the way people think and talk. I didn't take a course for that. I just spent time hanging out with people!

There's an old business axiom, *don't let the things you don't have prevent you from using the things you do have.* And that's one of the points I'm trying to make. You don't have to be a pro to be successful. Because when you achieve success, you become the standard.

Here's what I mean by that: when I wrote my first three books and couldn't get anyone to buy them, many readers thought they were shocking, lewd, and disgusting. Fast forward to present day. Those same books have sold more than 600,000 copies. Now they're "highly original!" "deliciously bawdy!" "highly addictive!" Last year I was amateurish, sophomoric, completely unskilled. Now I'm "brilliant!" "a genius!" "a gifted storyteller!"

You don't have to have a lot of experience and you don't have to be a great author. You just have to write well enough to sell lots of books. Believe me, the more you sell, the more talented you'll become in the eyes of the public!

It's not cheap to self-publish. Is it really worth the cost and effort?

If you have to ask, the answer is no!

You have to treat your writing like a business. Your book either has potential or it doesn't. If you believe it does, it's worth your investment. If you're not sure, and need someone else to tell you it's good, it belongs in the trash. I sent the *Saving Rachel* manuscript to a writer and an editor to get their take on it. The author said it might be the worst book ever written. The editor said it would never sell.

I published it anyway. Had I listened to the experts, I'd have missed out on the experience of what it's like to top the sales charts. In September, *Saving Rachel* sold 16 copies. Since then, more than 300,000! It was highlighted in *The Wall Street Journal*. It made *The New York Times* Best Seller List!

Where do you get your confidence? How did you know you were going to be successful as an author?

I felt I was successful the minute I finished writing a book I was willing to invest in. Most author hopefuls won't consider themselves successful until they've been validated by a publisher. To me, that shows lack of confidence. I've seen it a million times in the business world. Most people who want a bank loan go into a bank asking, "What do I have to do to get this loan?" Others enter a bank and ask, "What are you willing to do to get my business?"

It's all about attitude. If you think you're less of an author because you're self-published, you're going to write that way, and in my opinion, you can't develop a following unless you write with confidence. People might not like my writing, but they can't say it lacks confidence!

Will you read my book and give me your opinion? Or write a review or blurb for it?

No. And please don't ask, because it makes me uncomfortable to have to tell you no. If this book sells 10,000 copies and everyone wants me to read their book and write a review, what am I going to do? And how can I read some, and not others? I love you, I truly do, but the answer is no. But I'll teach you how to get reviews and blurbs in Part Two.

Why do you price your books at 99 cents?

It works for me because of the size of my target audience. You need to find the number that works for you.

Will you ever raise your prices?

Probably. But if I do, I'll almost certainly give my loyal followers a two or three-week window to buy at the lowest-possible "friendship" price, because they brought me to the dance, and this is one of the ways I can keep expressing my gratitude.

How does it feel to have a best selling book?

It feels damn good! You knew it would, and it does.

Will you ever go full-time as a writer?

No. I'd rather whine and complain about how I never have enough time to write.

Have you been approached by big name publishers?

Of course. But working for someone else wouldn't be fun for me.

Are you claiming everyone who follows your system can be successful?

Yes. But you might have to work harder at certain things than I did. I already mentioned I had no experience as an author, and never took any writing courses. But I had experience writing speeches. I was, in fact, good at it. But when I first started public speaking, I was terrible. So you know what I did?

I learned how to be better.

Can everyone learn how to be a better speaker? Of course! Can everyone become a great speaker? Yes, if they have an original style, a specific action plan and are willing to work hard enough.

When I decided to start writing, I was dreadful. Absolutely dreadful. So bad, even I knew it! And if you're just starting out, you're probably dreadful too. But I was willing to learn how to get better. I had already decided *Killing Hailey* wasn't good enough to publish. I had my own views about why it sucked, but I wanted a publishing editor's opinion of my strengths and weaknesses as a writer. I paid for a full-scale evaluation of the manuscript I already knew was terrible! It took about six weeks and cost $2,000. And the editor showed me why she thought my manuscript was dreadful. And I set it aside for a couple of weeks and pouted. But then I went to my computer and started a new story, concentrating on my strengths.

Wait—was the publishing editor a successful author?

Haha—no! But you know what? The world's greatest athletes hire trainers and teachers who aren't as good as they are. I once saw Jack Nicklaus getting a golf lesson when he was at the top of his game. Teachers and trainers and editors may not be able to tell you how to do something great, but they can tell you if you're doing something terribly wrong. I didn't hire this editor to teach me how to write. I hired her to tell me my strengths and weaknesses.

What if you don't have $2,000 to spend on a professional evaluation?

No problem. But you're going to have to work that much harder if you plan to get better on your own. Personally, I learned a lot from that initial, brutal evaluation. I changed some things and kept others as they were. I learned what she thought I was doing well, and learned what she felt my weaknesses were. And believe me, there were a lot more weaknesses than strengths! I had two pages of strengths and 17 pages of weaknesses!

I wasn't trying to become a great writer. I simply wanted to be an effective one. You might be a better author than me, and I hope you are. But my strength lies in knowing how to find an audience for the books I'm capable of writing.

If you ask anyone who knew me when I started, he or she will tell you the same thing: I have never taken myself seriously as a writer, but always felt I'd be able to write effectively enough to acquire and keep 10,000 loyal fans. I always believed I would outsell better authors the same way I outsold better salespeople when I was a kid: by loving my customers more, and never giving up on myself.

What Didn't Work!

One of the devices that makes the *American Idol* TV show successful is allowing the viewers to see the bad auditions first. I'll cover the good decisions I made in Part Two, because they became part of my marketing plan. But before I learned how to "sell a bunch by lunch and be a winner by dinner," I made a lot of terrible decisions that cost me a year of time and more than $25,000! Here are some of the worst:

> *I listened to others tell me how to market my books*
> *I tried to get into bookstores*
> *I tried to get interviewed by newspapers*
> *I hired a publicist*
> *I sent out press releases*
> *I did radio interviews*
> *I advertised my books in various media*

I know many of you are going to look at my list of "terrible" decisions and get upset with me. You'll write and tell me you've done those things and they turned out to be good decisions.

Fine. Write your own book!

I'm not saying mine is the only way, I'm just telling you what worked for me, and what didn't. And I can tell you my bad decisions got me no sales and cost me a fortune. The only good thing about them was I learned what didn't work for me.

I listened to others.

This is a strange one for me to write, because here I am, asking *you* to listen to *me*! I mean, if you shouldn't listen to others, why should you listen to me?

What I'm really saying is when I first tried to market my books I had no experience. I had a few ideas based on a lifetime of selling other products, but felt it would be the height of arrogance to assume I could do a better job than the "experts." So I spent a year trying all the traditional methods of selling my books, and none of them worked. I tried some hybrids, and those didn't work either. I kept great records, and can tell you what my sales were before and after each marketing campaign.

Though none of the traditional methods worked for me, I don't regret trying them. Anytime you're attempting something new it makes sense to try what the experts recommend, at least till you know better. At that point it's your responsibility as a marketer to come up with a better plan.

Practically everything works for someone, so I'm not saying the experts are wrong. I'm just saying they were wrong for me. The next few items were recommended to me by a number of experts, and I'll explain what I tried and why it didn't work for me.

Bookstores.

I won't bore you with details. I got one or two of my books in three local stores and my publisher got one of my books in another store. But it wasn't worth the effort. I don't know what I was thinking, but it was a dumb move based on the time and hassle factor. I'll make this short: bookstores don't want self-published authors on their shelves. You've had great luck? I'm happy for you. But it didn't work for me, so it goes in the "no" pile.

Newspaper Interviews.

Let's be clear: newspaper interviews are fantastic! The only problem is I was never able to get one. I contacted hundreds, but never got an interview. I've been at it all this time and I scored my very first newspaper interview this week! But they contacted me. I was recently featured in a story by the Wall Street Journal, but again, *they* contacted *me*. That distinction is important, because the reason I'm placing newspaper interviews in the "didn't work" pile is because all the letters and press releases I sent out, and all the phone calls I made yielded not one interview. I came close a couple of times, but they never pulled the trigger because I was a self-published author. They believed (rightfully so) if they did an article on me, they'd be flooded with requests from every self-published author in America! Forget interview or featured article! I never even managed to get a newspaper to *review* one of my books! The answer was always the same: "We don't review self-published books." If you've been interviewed or had your book reviewed in a print newspaper, congratulations. But it never worked for me until this week.

I hired a Publicist.

I didn't just hire a publicist, I hired the very best publicist in the business! But even he couldn't overcome the fact I was self-published. I paid him $2,500 a month for three months. Had I been a published author, I have no doubt he could have taken me to the top. I mean, this guy is *really* good! But he and I were climbing a steep hill. During those three months I had no increase in sales, which means I experienced virtually no sales! I don't want to imply I got nothing for my money. My publicist worked hard on my behalf. He composed and sent out tens of thousands of press releases, personally contacted studio executives, newspapers, radio and other outlets. He managed to get me several good reviews and five radio interviews (more on these in a minute). But none of these things translated into book sales.

Press Releases.

I've sent out tons of them! Two different agencies sent out several different press releases, and I sent out a couple on my own. Didn't matter who sent them or what was sent. Not a single sale can be traced to any of these press releases, and I received not a single response. We hit every possible combination of newspapers, TV, radio, human interest...you name it! In all, more than 100,000 press releases have been sent on my behalf.

> **Funny story:** Exactly a year after my publicist and I parted ways very amicably, *Saving Rachel* hit #1 on Amazon/Kindle. All of a sudden, my former publicist received numerous emails and phone calls from agents and publishers trying to locate me. How did they find him? Seems they all had my press release in their files! I assumed agents and publishers toss press releases in the trash, but they don't. They apparently file and archive them! And when they did in-house computer searches on John Locke they learned they could've had me for a phone call a year earlier!

Radio Interviews.

I know many of you love radio interviews. I don't. They stress me out, and I don't like them because I'm totally at the mercy of the host, who has almost certainly not read my book, and whose interview voice is hard for me to hear. If I'm talking to you face to face, I'm a pretty fair salesperson.

But anyone who knows me will tell you I don't like phones, and I especially don't like live phone interviews! In my experience, talk radio hosts have similar styles and agendas and are basically filling time. They're nice people, but many have a way of making all the interviews sound alike. I really hate when they ask for sample questions in advance, then fail to ask them. One radio host asked for five or six questions in advance, so I sent them, and spent two hours practicing my answers. When I got on the phone, he asked none of those questions. Instead, he spent half the interview asking my opinion about Tiger Woods' mistresses!

Radio salespeople claim they have thousands of listeners who buy fiction books, but I doubt that. I never listen to talk radio unless I'm in my car, and I can't remember reaching for a pen to jot down the name of a fiction book. The odds that someone will listen to your 5 minute radio interview and then purchase your book, are, in my experience, zero. Because after five radio interviews, including three regional and two national ones, I made zero sales. That said, I *do* believe listeners might buy a non-fiction book based on a radio interview.

Advertising.

I tried *everything!* Here are just a few:

I rented a huge kiosk in front of a Borders Bookstore in the local mall. It was six feet high and showed a picture of my book, *Lethal People*, along with a bunch of great reviews. I assumed Borders would carry my book since I was advertising it right in front of their store, but no. They even refused to order the book for the customers who entered the store asking for it. I know, because I sent people there to ask for it! I met the manager and offered to give her 10 free books and said they could keep 100% of the sales. They still refused! Although my ad remained there for several months, my sales remained flat!

I placed a $1,500 ad for *Saving Rachel* in the online daily, HARO (Help a Reporter Out). HARO is "the largest source repository in the world," and proclaims, "Advertising on HARO is the most cost effective way to reach a ridiculously large and targeted audience who actually listens and is looking for what you're promoting and selling." After reading testimonials that promised amazing results, I gave it a shot. I was told by their advertising department that HARO's ads are so effective, they wouldn't even allow me to craft the sales pitch, because they knew what would generate the maximum response. Well, I'm not saying their claims are false, I'm just saying it was a complete bust for me. I received not a single sale. And I mean, not one!

I paid thousands of dollars to create and show a movie trailer at 18 theaters before every R rated movie during the two week premier of Ironman II. This was a bust for several reasons, but I did get some name recognition. In other words, the trailer for *Saving Rachel* was seen and heard by up to twenty thousand people. They didn't buy, but it was branding. Nevertheless, it was very expensive, and not cost-effective. It *was* very cool, however!

There were many other bad advertising decisions, but you get the idea. These were all expensive efforts that sounded good at the time. I did them so you won't have to. Just think of all the money I saved you!

I also made some decisions that were neither good nor bad, such as creating book trailers. While they didn't pay for themselves, they're cool to have on my website, and I feel they lend professionalism. They may help visitors stay on my website a bit longer, and again, there's a certain cool factor that can't be ignored, if you can afford it. But if we're talking about business decisions, book trailers are an indulgence, not a necessity.

As we conclude Part One, let me just say...

You're about to learn what I did and how I did it. And it's not that I do so many different things than other people, it's that I do a few of the same things very differently. For one thing, I have a purpose for every action. Whether writing or marketing my books, every action I take is pre-determined. But the key to my success is I write to a specific audience (niche), and know how to find them (target marketing).

I take a complete, 100% business approach to my writing and selling effort. I have a specific business plan, and I adhere to it.

Wait. I don't like to repeat myself because I value your time. But it strikes me you might have missed the significance of something I wrote. I just gave you the key to having a best-selling book. Here it is again:

I write to a specific audience, and know how to find them.

Could anything possibly be better than that?

Let's roll...

Part Two

WHEREIN WE DISCUSS . . .

The four keys to success.

What you're doing wrong.

What you should be doing.

JOHN LOCKE

The Four Keys to Success

The system I developed can be broken down into a simple outline (I won't hit each point here, because I'm going to cover them in the detailed outline in Part Three, titled, *The Business Plan*).

1.   ### Have a Plan

 a.   For writing books
 b.   For marketing them

2.   ### Know your Target Audience

 a.   Write to them
 b.   Blog to them
 c.   Email them
 d.   Build loyalty

3.   Take a Business Approach

    a.   How to write, publish, and price your books

    b.   Turn your books and characters into a brand

    c.   Think of your books as employees

    d.   Maximize your profits

4.   Use your Tools Properly

    a.   Your books
    b.   Your website
    c.   Twitter
    d.   Your Blog

You might scan this outline and think, *I've heard all this before! I'm already doing all this!*

Well, you're wrong.

You've never seen anything like what I'm about to show you! You think you understand blogging? I'm going to show you how a single 550-word blog changed my life overnight! I don't mean "overnight" in a general way. I mean it literally. One day I wrote the blog, the next day I was successful.

But don't rush ahead to find the blog, because it won't make sense unless you've read everything that comes before.

Especially, the section on *knowing your target audience.* Without a clear understanding of that concept, it would be impossible to write the type of life-changing blog I'm going to demonstrate.

JOHN LOCKE

What You're (*Probably*) Doing Wrong

IF YOUR BOOK is decent and you're not selling lots of copies I know exactly what you're doing wrong. It's one or all of these four things:

You didn't have a plan for writing your book.
You didn't have a plan for marketing it.
You don't know who your target audience is.
You don't know how to find them.

If you don't have a plan for writing and marketing your books, the *only* way you can become successful is by pure chance!

Luckily, I know how to solve your problems.

The tools you'll need:

If you have a book, a website, a Twitter account, and a blog, you've got the right tools. You just need to learn how to use them in the most productive manner possible!

Bear with me as we go through the following pages, because explaining what you've done wrong and what you need to do is a process. Here's what you should have done from the beginning:

Have a Plan for Writing and Marketing Your Books:

The best way to write a best-selling book is to know who your audience is (and what they want) before you start writing. You should know everything there is to know about your readers in advance, and *then* write your book. Most people do it backwards. They write a book, then try to figure out how to market it. Most authors have never heard the words "target audience" or "target marketing," so their book-selling efforts amount to shooting in the dark and hoping to hit something.

What's a target audience? It's a tiny niche out of all the book buyers in the world. Imagine you're standing in a giant field in the middle of the night with a gun, and there are 20,000 targets all around you, but only one will make you successful. You have one bullet. What are your chances of hitting that single target?

Virtually zero.

But that's how most people are trying to market their books! They're just throwing them around in the marketplace like a guy throwing t-shirts into the stands at a basketball game, completely random, hit-or-miss. No wonder these authors are having trouble building a fan base! **Step one:** know your audience. **Step two**: write *to* them, which means, *give them what they want!*

Take this book, for instance, *How I Sold 1 Million eBooks in 5 Months*. I knew exactly who my eBook audience was before I wrote the first word. My audience is *you*, meaning:

- *Self-published authors.*

- *Published authors whose books aren't selling.*

- *People who are considering writing a book, or have started one, and want to know how to market it.*

I'd be surprised if you don't fit into at least one of these three categories. If you don't, you're not part of my target audience, which means you'll probably give me a lousy review!

In addition to knowing *who* my audience is, I also know what they *want*: They want to become a best-selling author.

I also know the size of my target market: There are 700,000 self-published authors in America.

Is it starting to come together for you?

Can you see how easy it will be for me to market this book? I'm writing to authors. I don't have to shoot blindly in the dark. All I have to do is find a bunch of authors! If I told you your target audience was authors, don't you think you could find them?

It's the same with writing fiction. Figure out who your audience is, then write your book.

What if you've already written your book?

700,000 self-published authors in the world feel your pain. That's what people do: they write without purpose. Oh, I know you had a purpose to write a great book. But you probably didn't write to a specific audience. You wrote the book, then thought, *now what?*

Well don't worry. You're doing it the hard way, but all is not lost. What you've got to do is profile your niche audience the same way an FBI profiler decides what type of person committed the crime. Here are some ways to do that:

- *Study your book and try to determine what type of person it "speaks" to.*

- *Get your book into the hands of a wide variety of people, and figure out what those who LOVE it have in common.*

- *Survey those who loved your book and find out why.*

- *Instead of generalizing, ask people about specific scenes: what was your favorite scene, and why? How did that scene make you feel? Did a particular scene move you? In what way? Which scene did you like better, X or Y? Why?*

- *Determine which thematic elements in your book appeal to which people, and what traits those people share.*

Okay, I know that sounds confusing, but you're the one who did this backwards, after all. So now you're going to have to put forth some effort to figure out who your target audience is.

Are you beginning to understand why you might be having problems with sales? On the one hand, it's obvious to you that non-fiction is *always* written with a specific audience in mind. On the other hand, you decided to write your fiction book with *no* specific audience in mind! See what you're up against?

I mean, if you're writing a book about how to be a better golfer, you're not going to talk about ice skating, right? You know before you start that your audience is everyone who wants to improve their golf game! So you write to your target, not someone else's target, and you give them what they want!

You get the picture. I'll move along. Just understand that from now on, every action you take will have a specific purpose. And that purpose will be to find your target audience, write to them, and turn them into guaranteed buyers of your future books.

Maybe it will help if I tell you who my target audience is.

Know Your Target Audience:

Here's mine:

The people who love my books love everyday heroes. They are compassionate people who root for the underdog, but are drawn to the outrageous, and have a dry sense of humor. They are all ages, but a surprising number are professional men and women above age 50. More than 70% are women, which defies everything you would normally think when you read my books! My readers are much more intelligent than you might expect. Many are doctors, nurses, and business leaders. Many are retired military. At least three are movie producers. At least two are working actors. At least one is a famous Broadway producer. And one is a brain surgeon!

Those who like my books tend to be busy people who are frazzled and stressed out beyond the point of no return, just as I am. I started writing to help me unwind, and those who love my books are also seeking stress relief. They've read their share of high brow books, but these days they mostly read to relax with a fast-paced, breezy read that makes them laugh out loud at the insane actions and situations I present. My readers are smarter than my heroes, and they know it. But in every book there comes at least one moment when my hero says or does something that is so deep or well-thought, or so endearing, my readers have to smile and think, "Old Emmett is a bit more wily than I gave him credit for!"

My male readers want to be Donovan Creed and my female readers want to date him. The ladies don't want to marry him though, because he's a bad risk. But they feel he has potential, and that makes him endearing. If he could just find the right woman...

My readers love a quiet hero, and they like to see my heroes getting themselves into trouble. Above all, my readers love the banter between my main characters and the people they encounter. They love action novels that are light on narrative and heavy on dialogue. They like a smart ass, and like to see a hero in control, but they don't want him to have an easy time of it. They love the fact that both my heroes know so little about women. They like the fact that Donovan Creed does a bad job of impressing the "right" women, and that he fails a lot in his romantic quest. They like how he makes his bewilderment plausible without coming across as whining.

My readers like the small bit of research I do. They don't want to be educated, but they love to learn one or two unusual facts along the way they can pass along in conversations at dinner.

My readers are renegades. They like the things editors hate, including, (1) I offer light character descriptions, (2) almost no details about settings unless they're related to the action, (3) I talk to the audience right in the middle of scenes like the Marx Brothers used to do, and (4) I use contemporary references that date my work!

My readers like sexual situations and sexual banter, if funny, but don't want to hear all the sexual details. If there's a bomb going off it only needs to be plausible, meaning my readers don't require a detailed explanation of how it was created or wired. My readers know I don't take my books seriously and don't expect them to, either. They know I'm not trying to save the world or write meaningful literature kids will have to study in school someday. They know the sole purpose of my writing is to make them smile or laugh for a few hours on a day when they need it most, and they like that about me.

What does all this mean?

To you it probably means nothing, because you're looking for a specific category, like "authors" or "golfers." But to me it *is* a specific category. I know who they are and what they want. And I know exactly how to find them: through my book, my website, Twitter, and especially my blog! But even though I know who they are and what they want, I still need to attract them to my books, and that requires an action plan.

Fortunately, I've got one, and I'll show it to you in a little while. And when you see it, a light will go on in your head and it will be just as obvious to you as if my category was "authors" or "golfers." Having said that, I also know that when you try to replicate what I've done by doing your own analysis, you will have some problems at first. That's when you'll email me and I'll have to remind you I don't have time to mentor. I can point you in the right direction and tell you which tools to use, and how to use them. But you'll have to create the tweets and blogs that drive traffic to your website.

When defining your target audience you'll be like an FBI agent looking for a fugitive. How does he start? By listing any facts that will help him find the guy. Maybe he's a welder. Maybe he kidnapped his son from his ex-wife. Maybe the son is eight years old and suffers from asthma. The more he learns about the guy, the easier it is to find him. But you've got it easier than the FBI agent, because you're not trying to find just one welder. You want to find *all* welders, and you also want to find every parent who has a child suffering from asthma!

If that analogy doesn't work for you, don't dwell on it. Just trust that when you have a plan and a reason for your actions, the odds of success will shift dramatically in your favor.

What You Should Be Doing

Set goals!

What type of goals should you set? How high should they be? What's practical? What's realistic? What makes sense? Here's my take, based on a lifetime of setting and hitting goals:

**Your goals should be low enough to hit,
and high enough to matter!**

...And only you know what's high enough to matter. But the one goal you shouldn't try to set is a sales goal!

What? Yeah, I know. Sounds crazy, right? But you need to concentrate on things you can control. Do that, and sales will take care of themselves. If you're marketing effectively, your audience will eventually find you. And when they do, they'll hunt down your books and demand more!

My first marketing goal was to get five 5-star reviews. That's it. But you know what? It took me almost two months!

I never set sales goals. I set project goals:

- *Determine my target audience*
- *Complete a manuscript*
- *Write a book that will sell*
- *Get my book into print*
- *Create a website*
- *Create a blog site*
- *Do a blog interview*
- *Get 5 great reviews*
- *Build a mailing list of 25 people who will buy next book*
- *Get 100 quality Twitter followers*

You get the picture. Small, but attainable. And every time I hit a goal, I set another. I'd rather have lots of small successes than hope for a big one. A lot can happen to discourage you if you're waiting on a goal that's too high to hit within a reasonable time frame.

Quick story from my past: When I was a sales agent for an insurance company, our district manager used to do a chalkboard report every Monday morning. Each person in the sales force would walk to the front of the room and write on the chalkboard what his sales goal was for the upcoming week. Clyde always wrote the same thing: 100 sales, and everyone would cheer. Joe would write 101, and make a comment to Clyde, and everyone would applaud their friendly rivalry. I would go to the board and write 7, or 9, or 12. One day I wrote down 8 sales ($2,000 of volume) and a new agent raised his hand and said, "Why is John so negative?" And the sales manager said, "John's actually going to hit his goal." —It's true. I always hit my goal, because even though I was writing down sales, I was counting presentations. I knew how many I had lined up, knew how many I could arrange that week, and knew what my selling average was. So my sales were the result of having a goal to make a certain number of presentations. By the way, I never saw Clyde or Joe make a single sale during the months they were with the company. They failed because they didn't have a plan for selling insurance, just as many authors have no plan for selling books. When I became a sales manager I kept the chalkboard report, but instead of asking how many sales they planned to make each week, I asked them to write down how many presentations they promised to give. I knew the sales would be there if they made the presentations.

Join Twitter!

Twitter was huge for me in many ways, though I had no clue how incredible this platform could be at the time I joined. But that first year I learned how to attract large numbers of quality followers, got to know some wonderful, good-hearted people, and managed to turn my main character into a household name.

Later in the book I'll go into detail about how I use Twitter for maximum profit, but for now, let me make this point: Twitter cost me no money to join and my blog cost me very little. But these two platforms became the one-two punch that made my marketing successful. Everyone has access to Twitter and blogging. But people don't use these resources the way I think they should.

Develop a brand!

One of the best things I did in the early days before creating my marketing system was to develop my character into a brand name. Donovan Creed has become a brand, a franchise.

From the very start, People heard the name Donovan Creed so often, by the time they got around to reading my books it seemed he was already famous! Just this morning I received an email from a lady who wrote, "Tell Donovan I miss him!" I responded, "I gave Creed your message and he winked. What's *that* all about?" She emailed back, "LOL! Don't tell my husband!" —These silly remarks give my character the "feel" of being a real person. Honestly, I get several emails a day where people directly address my character. Even Kim Kardashian sent a happy birthday tweet to Creed once, but that's another story for another day!

www.DonovanCreed.com takes you to my website, and DonovanCreed.blogspot.com used to take you to my original blog, and DonovanCreed.wordpress.com used to take you to my second blog (now I'm set up to blog on my actual website). John@DonovanCreed.com is my email address, and @DonovanCreed is my twitter name. It's a consistent message.

When I began using Twitter more than a year ago, Creed and I had "conversations" that created a lot of Twitter buzz. I was the straight man and Creed was the sarcastic foil to my comments. I'm married, so I can't get away with flirting. But Creed was accepted for being mildly flirtatious! I eventually stopped tweeting that way because people were getting confused about which of us was real (the fact that John Locke was a huge character on the TV show *Lost* probably added to the confusion!) Since repetition builds impact, Donovan Creed is well on the way to becoming a household name.

When I realized *Saving Rachel* was my ticket to the big time, I did some Rachel branding as well. SavingRachel.com will also take you to my website, and when I did interviews I focused on *Saving Rachel* instead of sending a mixed message about the different books. I said, "Try *Saving Rachel*. If you don't like that one, you won't like the others."

Saving Rachel became the face of my writing style, and Donovan Creed became the face of my franchise.

Keep writing books!

This seems obvious to me, but when I talk to other authors about it, they often look at me like I've got two heads!

Apparently this is hard for people to believe, but I didn't even *try* to start marketing my books until I had published three of them! I hired the publicist as I was completing the fourth book. At the same time I was doing all the things the experts were recommending, I continued to write books. I had five titles published by the time I decided to create my marketing plan. And having five books available at the same time is probably the best thing I did right. Here's why:

> Most authors write a book and then do all they can to market that book. But what if your book is a huge success? Where are your readers going to go? You spent all that time and energy to acquire an audience that loves your writing, and there's no second, third and fourth book for them to buy! I have sales figures and emails to prove the vast majority of people who buy one of my books will buy one or more of the others. And many buy them all. I won't make you read a bunch of emails about it, but I want to show you a few sales numbers from the first five months of 2011 on Kindle alone.

Look how close each pair of sales is for these different books:

Wish List:	149,277
Lethal People:	149,103
Lethal Experiment:	107,921
A Girl Like You	106,720
Now & Then	95,981
Vegas Moon	95,962

Lethal People was my first novel, Wish List was my fifth! If I had stopped writing to promote Lethal People, my readers would have had nothing else to read! I would have lost out on all these other sales! And don't forget, Saving Rachel, my third book, sold 300,000 downloads during the same period!

Here's why having five books created incredible symbiosis in my marketing effort: when you publish your book on Amazon, the potential book buyer will see your book cover, plot synopsis, and reviews. If you've got only one book on Amazon, like *Lethal People*, you're putting all your eggs in one basket. 100% of your books will be judged by that one cover, plot, and reviews.

But I had five different covers, five different plots, and five sets of reviews! Five different ways to attract an audience! And here's something else you should know: readers prefer authors who have multiple titles. They like knowing there are more books available in case they love the first one.

Do you understand what I'm saying? You might look at the cover and plot synopsis of *Lethal People* and decide it's not your cup of tea. But tomorrow you might happen upon the cover and plot synopsis of *Wish List*, and think, "This sounds interesting. What the heck, I'll give it a try." If it turns out you love *Wish List*, you won't *care* what the cover or plot of *Lethal People* looks like, because now you trust the *author*! So tomorrow you'll eagerly purchase the book you passed on today!

Having five books out at the same time is a *huge* advantage to an author who has just been "discovered." What could be more frustrating to a reader than to fall in love with an author and be told he or she has to wait many months for the next book? You might be completely forgotten by the time you've written another book.

Create a website!

You need a website so you can have a "Contact Me" button. Everything else you put on there is gravy. Make sure your website is clean, sleek, and professional. When you're thinking about adding bells and whistles, calculate how long it might take people with older computers to load. It would be terrible to lose valuable contacts because you tried too hard to impress them!

Give interviews and participate in guest blogs!

Follow blogs, respond to them. Ask to be interviewed by the ones you enjoy. And the same goes for any opportunity you can find to be a guest blogger.

Here's what you shouldn't expect from doing interviews and guest blogs: lots of sales.

Here's what you're going for: name recognition. Branding. Getting your message out there, so it can be picked up by search engines!

I try to answer questions on guest blogs and interviews with quotable sound bites, so if someone types a subject into a search engine, my quote appears. For example, when I first saw I could make money selling eBooks for one-tenth the price famous authors were asking, I said, "I no longer have to prove my books are as good as the world's most famous authors'. Now they have to prove their books are ten times better than mine!" —I've seen that quote on dozens of Google search engines over the past year. *The Wall Street Journal* used it in the article about my sales! People like it, click on it, and are taken to the interview or guest blog where I said it. Once there, they'll see the link to my website, and my Contact button. From there, we're a step away from an email friendship. And I build my reading audience one email at a time!

I usually make anywhere from no sales to a half-dozen or so from each guest blog or website interview. Maybe you'll do better than me. But name recognition is very valuable, and gives you a chance to brand your books and franchise your main characters. Remember, everything you say in a blog lives forever, so it could take weeks or months for those comments to reach the right person's eyeballs!

There is also much to be said for the connections you'll make in the blogging community. You can probably score a blurb or two from those who buy your books. Could be their review is the one that influences ten others to buy your book. Maybe those ten will influence 100! This is why guest blogs and interviews are hard to quantify with a specific valuation. But they do have value and belong in your success arsenal.

I recommend you develop at least one highly-quotable remark for each interview or guest blog, and that you go into the encounter with a theme, and pound that theme over and over. For example, I did an interview where I tried to reduce every answer to how much FUN my books are! I've used one of the quotes from that interview several times since: "Opening *Saving Rachel* is like opening a box of fun. In fact, you don't even need to open it, because if *Saving Rachel* tips on its side, fun spills out!"

Being successful in interviews and blogs is a matter of being prepared, and having a plan for every action you take. If you have a plan for your interview or blog, you'll come out better than you went in. Some people say they prefer to go in "cold" and speak "off the cuff." I heard that a lot when I was doing public speaking. I often worked a week to write and deliver a five-minute speech, while others just stood up and spoke. I feel now as I did then: speaking "off the cuff" is another way of saying you didn't bother to prepare. And what does that say about the respect you have for your audience?

ePublish!

I didn't just ePublish, I ePublished at an "unfair" price, meaning, a price at which traditionally published authors can't compete!

I price my novels at 99 cents because it offers a crazy good value for the reader. I also understand the concept of pricing at $2.99, and have often considered it because you earn 70% commission at that price point instead of 35%. My decision came down to whether I thought I could sell seven times as many books at 99 cents as I could at $2.99. I felt I could, because my target audience was big enough. If your target audience is smaller than mine, you'll want to charge more money. Here's something else no one seems to understand about pricing eBooks: they argue back and forth about whether or not they should charge 99 cents or $2.99 or $4.99 or whatever. And they're basing it on how many books John Locke is selling at 99 cents, or how much money someone else is making by charging $2.99! Plain and simple, figure out the size of your target audience, then figure out how much you want to earn when you find them! In the case of this "How To" book, my target is 700,000 authors. If I had ten books to sell, like I do with my Donovan Creed and Emmett Love series, I'd offer this one for 99 cents, hoping to sell you nine more. But all I've got is the one "How To" book. So I'm charging what I have to in order to net the same amount of money I'd make if I were selling you ten books at 99 cents. Here's the math: I earn 35% on books that sell for 99 cents (35 cents profit), and 70% for books that sell for $4.99 ($3.50 profit).

10 fiction books X 35 cents royalty for each = $3.50 per customer.
1 non-fiction book X $3.50 royalty for each = $3.50 per customer.

See? Every decision is based on a plan, and every action has a purpose.

Love your readers and personally respond to them!

I absolutely adore my readers and they know it. I answer every email, even though doing so requires an enormous time commitment. I don't attempt to put a dollar figure on it, because one person could lead you to five, who lead you to twenty-five, and one of them might option your book for a movie. But apart from being a good business move, it's good manners, and I'm hopelessly grateful whenever someone cares enough about my books to write to me. I literally build my following one contact at a time, and these friends help me by spreading the word to their friends. It's a grass roots movement that costs time, but virtually no money. I love my readers, and I like to think they love me, too. I've seen many go to bat for me. Some defend me when I get a bad review from someone outside my target audience. If you've had this happen, I don't have to tell you how special it is!

Think of your books as employees!

I'm a businessman, and I look at each of my books as an employee. I consider my ten books (including this one) to be my international sales force. The seven (soon to be eight) Donovan Creed novels make up the Creed division. I also have a western division made up of the two westerns I've sent out into the world. My sales people have names: People, Experiment, Rachel, Now, Wish, Stone, Girl, Vegas, Bear, and I'll refer to this "How To" book as Howie.

You might think this is just me being cute.

It's not.

I take it all the way, and think of my books as living people. When I look at Rachel's sales report and see she sold 314 downloads in Europe last night while I was sleeping, I instinctively think, *Wow, great job, Rachel!* And if Rachel's sales are trending up, while Girl's are trending down, I consider writing my next book a little more like Rachel, and a little less like Girl.

I make a one-time investment in each of these "employees" of a few thousand dollars (production costs including formatting, editing, cover design, etc.) and then I send them out into the world to make sales.

As in any business, some salespeople do better than others. For several glorious weeks my first eight "salespeople" were among the top 50 on Amazon/Kindle! Obviously, as each salesperson makes more sales, his market becomes more saturated. As of this morning, Vegas has been working for seven weeks, and has brought in about 105,000 sales from all sources. Several days she brought in more than 5,000! Yesterday, only 800. It's natural that as she makes more sales, her saturation point increases. Good thing there are more and more readers buying Kindles and other devices each year! Hopefully, Vegas will continue to attract new sales for many months and years to come. She will almost certainly never sell more than 5,000 a day again unless a movie is made, but that's okay. It only took her seven days to reimburse me for all the expenses it took to hire her! Every sale she made after the seventh day was pure profit, and every sale she continues to make will be profit, day after day, month after month, year after year.

As of this writing, I have nine sales people (you're reading the tenth), and they are all among the top 105 sales people on Amazon/Kindle! By the time you read this, those nine salespeople will no longer be among the top 100. But they'll be making *some* sales, and the sales they generate will be at no expense to me. It's like an annuity that has repaid the initial investment, and every dollar is a bonus at this point.

Vegas has netted me more than $30,000 profit after expenses in two months on the job. But unlike a real employee, I don't have to deal with her in person, or on a daily basis. I don't have to match her social security or provide benefits. I don't have to worry that she's not working, or wonder if she's interviewing with my competition. I don't have to keep track of her sick days, or take her phone calls. I don't have to worry if she got her feelings hurt, or if she's upset with her husband, or if she has a drinking, drug, or gambling problem. She works tirelessly, 24 hours a day for free (at this point), and will continue to do so for the rest of her electronic life.

—How can these eBooks not be the best investment in the world?

Develop a list of guaranteed buyers!

My ultimate goal is to have an email list of 10,000 guaranteed buyers. Am I close? No. But I didn't start with a goal of 10,000. I started with a goal of 25. Then I raised it to 100. Then 250. Then 500. Then 1,000. I've hit all those, and now I'm working on 2,500. Bear in mind, these aren't friends and family, or author friends, or names on a mailing list. These are my OOU's (more on this near the end of the book), people who have told me they are fans for life, and will buy anything I write!

Can you imagine anything more powerful than having an email list of 10,000 people who will buy anything you write? Let me put it another way: 1,000 guaranteed buyers can propel a book into the Top 100, if they not only buy, but spread the word to all their friends!

How do I know?

Follow the Stone, a *Western*, hit the Top 100 in 14 days.
A Girl Like You hit the Top 100 in 10 days.
Vegas Moon hit the Top 100 in 7 days.
Don't Poke the Bear! Hit the top 100 in 7 days

When I publish a new book I send an email to 250 of my loyal fans each day and ask them to spread the word. Because they're loyal fans, they tell all their friends and family members. Each day my books move up the sales chart dramatically. After several days of sending these notices to key people, I'm on the Top 100.

Once you hit the Top 100, you no longer have to find people. *They* will find *you!*

Target Marketing.

It's fitting that the list of what you should be doing ends with Target Marketing, because this is the solution to all your book-selling problems, assuming your book doesn't suck. In the next few pages I'll explain the concept in detail. In Part Three, I'll show you exactly how I used my books, my website, Twitter, and my blog to sell more than a million eBooks in five months.

Back to target marketing. First, the definitions:

- Selling downloads is nothing more than writing to a specific audience, and knowing how to find them.

- Your specific audience is your niche.

- Finding your niche is called target marketing.

Don't worry about selling them. I've told you several times sales isn't your goal. In the insurance business the goal wasn't sales, it was presentations. Getting a prospect to SEE my product. If you can get your book in front of your target audience, a high percentage will buy. What's a high percentage? To me, anything above 10% is high.

I've made two serious fortunes in my life, and I'm not counting book sales. And both those fortunes were created from scratch, in businesses where everyone I knew was struggling at the time. I succeeded because I created a selling system that worked. The success I've had as an author came right in the middle of the worst economic period our country has faced in many years, a time when most of the authors I met were struggling to make sales. I succeeded in selling books the same way I succeeded in business: I created a selling system that worked.

Okay, let's do this together.

A niche.

I write those words and get goose bumps. Crazy, right? But check it out: every success story in the world happened because someone found a niche. And nine times out of ten, when they tried to expand outside that niche, they failed.

One reason I didn't accept a major publishing contract for my Creed series is because I knew the publishers would want to maximize their sales. That makes sense, right? For them, yes. But it doesn't make sense for me.

Here's why: my Donovan Creed character is an edgy guy. If you haven't read my books you'll have to take my word for it that Creed is not a *Little House on the Prairie* kind of guy. If a major publisher gives me a $2 million advance for my next four books, and does a major ad campaign, at some point they're going to say, "We're getting negative feedback on your titles. You need to soften your characters a bit, to appeal to a wider audience." They'll say, "You have this habit of having your character talk to your audience, and our research shows this is distracting and annoying to 80% of all readers." They'll say, "Your language is crude and offensive, and we've been getting complaints your subject matter is not just inappropriate, but completely off the charts!" —And the next thing you know, they're going to be changing the very formula that made my books successful among my niche in the first place.

There's an audience for my Creed books, but it's not a wide one. There are NOT a million eBook readers who would love my books! Not even close. The publisher's feed-back would be 100% correct! Of *course* four out of five readers won't like my books! I'm not writing for those people! I'm only writing for the *cool* readers! ☺

In my opinion, understanding whom your target audience is, and what they want, and writing to them (and only them!) is the most important component of being successful as an author.

You've probably been thinking all this time how great it would be to have your book read and loved by millions of people all over the world. I'm not saying that's impossible, but the odds are against you. Consider this book. It's a niche book with information highly specific to one tiny segment of the reading public. It would be ridiculous for me to expect a million people to want to read this book. The *only* people likely to enjoy it are authors who want to sell more books. In other words, there are no "feel good" Oprah moments. No recipes. No photos of movie stars. No romance. No car chases. No zombies or werewolves. It is definitely *not* something for everyone.

Just as this book is written for a specific audience, so are all my novels written to a specific niche. The Creed books are a different niche than my Emmett Love western novels. While there is some cross-over from the Creed fans, the marketing "angle" for my western books requires a more subdued, nostalgic flavor.

My dedicated Creed audience is slightly above 100,000 people. How stupid would I be to "tone down" my characters, and write more politically correct story lines and scenes in hopes of reaching a million readers! If I change my characters and story lines to widen my audience, I'll lose my dedicated core audience, the ones who brought me to the dance, the ones who want to buy my future books.

I can see where that comment might confuse you because I have sold over a million books. But I only sold that many because most of my readers bought several different John Locke novels!

Remember what I said a little while ago? I'm repeating it because repetition builds impact: every success story in the world happened because someone found a niche. And nine times out of ten, when they tried to expand outside that niche, they failed. So if I try to expand my niche by softening my tone, I'll lose my core audience, because the very thing that makes my writing unique to them will have been taken away.

That doesn't mean I can't have more than 100,000 hard-core readers. I have another 20,000 who love my westerns! I believe I can build this group up to 50,000 over time. My first western has sold over 50,000 during the past three months, and the second one has only been out a few weeks. But when I'm talking about a core group, I'm talking about loyal fans who will buy *everything* I write in a certain genre. And I think I've got about 20,000 right now who will buy my next western with nothing more to go on than seeing or hearing it has been released.

In the years ahead, as millions more people buy reading devices, perhaps my Creed books could get to 200,000 fans or more. But my target market is only about 100,000 readers at this moment. I understand and accept this, and knew it going in.

This is a hard concept to explain, because I've already told you *Saving Rachel* has sold more than 300,000 copies. You could argue that proves my target audience is at least 300,000 readers. But you'd be wrong. Most of those readers were not part of my target audience. They bought *Saving Rachel* because it was the number one book on Amazon/Kindle. If pressed for an answer, I would guess maybe 180,000 of those 300,000 enjoyed the book. But that doesn't make them hard-core fans.

If you want more readers than you can get by writing to your niche, you'll need to create a second stream of income—a DIFFERENT niche. That's why I created my western series of Emmett Love novels. It's a whole different niche. I can build a separate loyal audience for that series without screwing up the Creed franchise.

I want a DEEP fan base, not a WIDE one. I'd rather have 100,000 fiercely loyal fans than two million who "try and buy" and turn out to be "one and done." You might be happy to sell two million copies and not care that you have no truly loyal readers. But not me. I had a fan who wrote me last month, said he was a war veteran, loved my books, ended his email saying he'd take a bullet for me.

A bullet.

Maybe in real life he wouldn't actually take a bullet for me. But when a Viet Nam vet tells you he will, it's a sign of serious loyalty.

You might not want rabid fans. But I do. And if you do too, I'll show you how to attract and keep them, and this will turn out to be one of the big keys to your success.

I think I can prove to you (if I must) that the VAST majority of the people who have read three Donovan Creed books will read EVERY Donovan Creed book. I don't have an exact statistic, but I'm fairly certain 30% of the people who read *Saving Rachel* hated it, another 20% were ambivalent, 20% mildly enjoyed it, and 30% loved it. The haters and those who were ambivalent never bought a second Creed. Half of those who enjoyed it bought another Creed, and those who loved it bought every Creed book. If I were to go on a morning talk show to promote my Creed books, a staggering percentage of the viewers would probably hate them, because the people who are attracted to those types of shows are generally not my target audience. I mean, obviously some of them would be, but I'd rather go on a show where a high percentage of viewers would like my books. It's like this "How To" book. I could go on Oprah to promote it, but what percentage of her viewing audience would be a candidate to buy it? On the other hand, if I went to a writer's convention and spoke about this book, an astronomically high percentage of attendees would be likely to buy.

So how do you figure out whom your target audience is? –That's the toughest part. Some types of books are obvious: cook books, celebrity books, paranormal, sci-fi, young adult, "How To" books, etc. Some are harder: mystery, thriller, romance books, etc.

You might wonder why a romance book's audience might be harder to pin down than a science fiction book's audience. Good question, and I'm not sure I can give you a reasonable answer! But I think the science fiction audience is much narrower, and the more you can narrow your audience, the more success you're likely to find in marketing (I know that probably sounds incredibly weird to you!)

Maybe a better example is paranormal, which trends toward a specific age group, while romance is all over the board. If I were selling romance, I'd try to create a sub category in the genre in order to narrow my target audience.

This is a hard concept for authors to understand. Most people are wired to ask, "How can I maximize my audience?" My recommendation is to narrow your audience as much as possible, in order to create a specific niche. If two million eBook readers like romance books, I'd want to write the type of romance book that appeals to 10% of that market in a huge way. Because those 200,000 fans will be extremely loyal, and they'll buy your future books. Not only that, these people will have a circle of influence that will be responsive to your unique style of writing, because friends tend to like the same things.

The best way to find your target audience is to write something original! When you're truly original, the mainstream readers of that genre will often consider your work outrageous, or shocking, or insane, or unique, or weird, or all these things, but that's okay. If it's your original voice, stand proud and pick one of your books to slam down the throats of the entire obvious audience. Then be strong enough to deal with the high percentage of hate reviews you will certainly get from those who don't "get" your work. A lot of authors can't handle hate reviews. But a bad review simply means someone outside your target audience found your book. The angrier the review, the further removed from your target audience they are. But along with the hate reviews, you'll get some great ones.

The reason you'll get some great reviews for your original writing is because I don't care what you're selling, there's a market for it! What I'm saying, if you're not offending a significant number of readers, your writing is probably not very original. And the less original you're writing, the less loyal your fan base will be.

Saving Rachel went out into the world to pave the way for my other books. She got all beaten and bloody in order to help me find my target audience, what I lovingly refer to as the cool people! When she found the cool people, they bought my other books. If you check the reviews for my books you'll see that *Saving Rachel* has the worst percentage of positive ratings. That's because a higher percentage of my fans bought the other books.

While we're on the subject, let me tell you how I track reviews. Amazon reviews go in whole numbers, from one to five stars. I throw out the 3-star reviews, count the 1 and 2-star reviews as negative, and the 4 and 5-star reviews as positive. Then I divide those by the total number.

Example: As of this writing, *Saving Rachel* has 231 four and five star reviews, and 155 one and two star reviews. That totals 386 reviews (again, I don't count the 38 three star reviews, since they're neither positive or negative). By dividing the positive by the total number, I get a score of 59.8% positive reviews. You might think that's terrible, and it would be, if all my books had that number. But let's look at the others:

Lethal People: 67.4% positive (this was my first book. I was still learning my craft)

Wish List: 72.8% positive (Creed appears in less than half of this book)

Now & Then: 74.4% positive (Creed appears only in the first half of this book)

Vegas Moon: 84.2% positive

A Girl Like You: 84.4% positive

Lethal Experiment: 90.7% positive (Does this mean *Lethal Experiment* is better written than my other books? No. It just means it has been reviewed by a higher percentage of my target audience than the other books).

And my westerns:

Follow the Stone: 88.6% positive

Don't Poke the Bear: 84.2% positive

I just checked the list of the top 10 books on Amazon/Kindle and saw the famous authors' percentages were all over the board. The highest was 90.2% positive. The lowest was 48.0% positive. So I'm feeling pretty good about my numbers.

Okay, here you go. I think you're going to love this next part.

Part Three

WHEREIN WE DISCUSS . . .

The Business Plan

The System, Step by Step

How to Write a Life-Changing Blog

Building Loyalty

Business Plan Outline

Here is the business plan that will make you successful:

1. <u>Write the best and most original book you can.</u>

   a. Put your best reviews at the front.

   b. Create recurring characters that will drive a series.

   c. Create memorable "water cooler" scenes.

   d. Display your website and blog site URL's before and after your story.

2. <u>Create a website.</u>

    a.   Use Twitter to create a Friendship Circle.

    b.   Drive your Twitter friends (and book readers) to your website.

    c.   Drive them to your "Contact Me" button.

    d.   Personally email them.

    e.   Convert them into loyal friends.

    f.   Convert your loyal friends to buyers.

    g.   Convert the buyers to reviewers.

    h.   Put them on your Guaranteed Buyer mailing list.

    i.   Email them to promote your next book.

3. <u>Create a simple, no-nonsense blog site.</u>

    a.   Post short, infrequent, *Loyalty Transfer* blogs to your Target Audience that showcase your writing ability and unique style. Make sure your reader has a link to your book(s) near the end of each blog post.

4. <u>Promote your blog</u>.

    a. Use Twitter to generate buzz and create leads.

    b. Use Twitter search and hash tags to create a Viral Circle.

    c. Drive your Twitter friends (and book readers) to your blog site.

    d. Convert the viewers to blog subscribers.

    e. Convert the subscribers to loyal friends, book buyers and review writers.

    f. Put them on your Guaranteed Buyer mailing list.

    g. Email them to promote your next book.

5. <u>ePublish your book.</u>

    a. Use Social Media to generate buzz and leads and drive traffic to your website and blog site so you can continue fueling the Friendship Circle.

6. <u>Repeat the cycle with future books.</u>

Take a few minutes to study this as if it were a painting. I'm serious. If you don't, you may not appreciate its beauty. There are two steps in this Business Plan Outline that can take you viral, and get you hundreds, perhaps thousands of sales in a matter of days. They're the two steps that made me successful overnight.

Please. Read over the Business Plan Outline one more time, because I'm about to break it down for you, step by step, and it will come together much better if you read it again.

Please. I'm trying to help you here, so humor me. Read the Business Plan Outline a second time, slowly, so the next part will flip a switch in your brain and give you that "Aha!" moment you crave.

Okay.

By the way, the two steps I created that made all the difference to my sales are 3.a. and 4.b.

Go back and read 3.a. and 4.b.

I'll wait.

You're not impressed, right? Well let me tell you something. When I finish describing them to you, you're going to break into a grin. If you have even the most rudimentary understanding of marketing, you will smile. By the time you finish reading my explanation of 3.a. you'll see why I would have gladly paid $10,000 for this one idea alone!

And you're getting it for $4.99 eBook, $9.99 paperback!

The System, Step by Step

THE FIRST STEP talks about sending a book into the world to divide readers into two camps. This is one of the things you need to do if you don't already know your target audience. When I wrote *Saving Rachel*, I was not following the system I later developed, so I was in the same boat you're probably in, meaning, I wasn't certain who my target audience was yet.

1.   Write the best and most original book you can.

This is your **Target Book**, your *Saving Rachel*. This is the book you're going to send out into the world to find your **Target Audience**. Yes, *Saving Rachel* was my third book, but when I wrote it, I realized it would be the key to finding my target audience, because it divided people like crazy. Most either hated it or loved it. If I had known then what I know

now, *Saving Rachel* would've been my first book. But that's not important. What's important is that you write a unique, original book that will divide the reading world into two camps: those who love your writing and those who hate it. Those who hate it will give you angry, spiteful reviews. That's the bad news. The good news is they'll never buy your books again, so that will end their angry reviews!

I know what you're thinking: *"Why is alienating half the book buying audience a good thing?"* The answer is it proves you're original. And the more unique and original your writing, the deeper and more loyal your target audience will be. I mean, there's a limit—you don't want *everyone* to hate your work! Ideally, you'd hope for 60% to love your Target Book, 30% to hate it, and you'll always have 10% who can't decide, which means they're probably open to trying another of your books.

Once you know your target audience you'll write directly to them. If you don't get a lot of bad reviews with your Target book, you're not original enough. I'm not talking about your initial reviews. Almost all of those will be positive. I'm talking about the reviews you get after your book starts moving up significantly. That's when the bad reviews start creeping in. But that's a good thing because it will help you identify and grab the attention of your Target Audience.

1.a.   Put your best reviews at the front.

Before your story starts, you should display your best reviews for the book. Not long paragraphs, but short blurbs and hard-hitting one- or two-sentence reviews. By doing that, you're calling forth your witnesses. Every review gives your audience another reason to like your book before they start reading it. You're getting your readers into the proper frame of mind for a positive experience.

1.b. Create recurring characters that will drive a series.

People like to read books about characters they know and like. If you manage to create a character that rocks, your readers will feel comfortable the next time they open a book featuring that character. After a couple of books, it'll be like "old home week" for your readers. Why go to all the time and trouble to create new characters if your readers want more stories about your existing ones?

After you've written a book with several great characters, the next one will take half the time to write because your main characters are already in place, and you have a good feel for them. My cast of recurring characters in the Donovan Creed series obviously includes Donovan Creed. Callie Carpenter is often featured. Rachel Case gets regular billing. There are more than a dozen other characters that move in and out of the different books. I always introduce several new characters to play off the "stars," but my readers would be disappointed if I kept writing books with all new characters and none of the established ones. If you want to take a break from the series, do what I did: create another series. I have a whole different set of characters for my western novels that feature former gunslinger Emmett Love, and his love-interest, Gentry. Your readers will get to know your characters, and love them, and want to read more about them. And it's your job to give them what they want.

1.c.   Create memorable scenes.

Are you familiar with the phrase "water cooler?" The idea is, people see, read, or hear something the night before they enjoyed so much they can't wait to talk about it while standing around the water cooler with their friends at the office the next day. These are the types of scenes you want to create in your books, scenes that create a buzz.

Examples:

If you've seen the movie *Deliverance*, all I'd have to say is, "What about that scene from *Deliverance*?" –And you know exactly what I'm talking about! And if you didn't, I could give you two clues from memory: "Squeal like a pig!" or, "He's got a pretty mouth!"

If you've seen the movie *Basic Instinct*, all I have to say is, "Sharon Stone, *Basic Instinct*," and your mind immediately conjures the famous scene where she crosses her legs during the police interview.

My favorite movie scene of all time is the Tango Scene in *Scent of a Woman*. If you've seen the movie, your mind takes you right to that incredible scene.

I haven't written universally famous scenes like these. But if you were to say to my readers, "*Vegas Moon*, Surrey the doll..." they would smile as they remember one of the most memorable scenes I have created.

You may like all, some, or none these scenes. But they are memorable, and someone's target audience will love all or some of them. My target audience will feast on #1, #2, and #4. But they wouldn't fawn over my personal favorite, the Tango Scene. However, in the same movie, *Scent of a Woman*, when Col. Slade is on the plane explaining to Charlie why he loves women—my target audience would *love* that scene! So if I were writing *Scent of a Woman* for my target audience, I'd feature more scenes like the plane scene and fewer like the tango scene, because I want to give my readers not what *I* like, but what *they* like. If I didn't know my target audience, I wouldn't know *what* types of scenes to write. I'd be writing blindly! Leaving my scenes and novels completely to chance! I did that early in my writing career, and got myself in trouble with my fourth novel, *Now & Then*, which alienated 20% of my loyal readers!

You might hate my Creed books. If you do, it doesn't mean you hate my writing, it simply means you're not part of my Donovan Creed target audience. You could like my westerns and hate my Creeds. Or vice-versa. Or like or hate both of them. But one thing you can count on is that I will stay true to my target audience. Regardless of the genre, I write solely for the entertainment of that specific audience. I write the types of scenes they like, and avoid the types of scenes I know they don't like. If I'm not sure about a scene, I sneak it in and get feedback from my readers after the fact, to make sure I'm staying true to the stories and characters they've come to enjoy reading.

As I mentioned, I took a hit from 20% of my core fans for the book *Now & Then*, so I dropped the story line on the spot, even though 60% of my feedback was highly positive. In all, 20% hated it, 20% were neutral, and 60% loved it (I'm not referring to my written Amazon reviews, I'm referring to the emails I received from my loyal fan base). These would be great stats if they'd come from the general public (75% positive – in fact the general public stats were identical: 74.4% positive). But you should never get 20% negative results from your hard core fans! My niche is not enormous, and I can't afford to drive a wedge between the fans I've cultivated. If I catered future books to the 60% who loved *Now & Then*, I'd lose up to 40% of my fan base. So I won't repeat the mistake. I learned my lesson. I won't write any more *Now & Then* type stories that feature Donovan Creed.

You might ask, "By not writing similar stories for the fans who loved *Now & Then*, aren't you taking a chance on losing them?" No. They were hardcore Creed fans before *and* after *Now & Then*. They might be disappointed I dropped the story line, but they still love all things Creed. If I'm married to a *Now & Then* type of story line, I will write that type of book with different characters, and warn my core fans ahead of publication. Then if they decide to read it, it's a choice they've made. You might think I'm nuts to do that, but I love my target audience, and want to protect them from a story they might not like, even if it's one I wrote!

Again, it's part of building a deep fan base instead of a wide one.

1.d. <u>Display your website and blog site URL's before and after your story</u>.

The purpose of this is obvious. You want to drive traffic to your website and blog site. It gives your readers a chance to keep thinking about you at the very moment you have their full attention. It's a call to action, and you should have something special waiting for them at both sites. Perhaps a blog that will move them or speak to their hearts, or a link to the Amazon review section, or a contest or promotion, or whatever you can come up with that would appeal to your readers.

2. <u>Create a Website</u>

Do you really need a website? Yes, you really do. Does it have to be expensive? No, it doesn't. I spent less than $500 for my first website and only $17.50 a month for hosting, and didn't upgrade until I had sold more than 850,000 downloads! It wasn't perfect, and it was cumbersome, and I had recurring problems trying to post on it, but I managed. If you can't afford a fancy website, use a template from one of the hosting companies, or pay a college kid who specializes in website creation to create one for you cheap. You need a website because it gives your customers a place to go where they can read about your background and any other information you want them to have, and most importantly, it gives them a Contact button so you can capture their name and email address, with a comment section where you can determine the level of their enthusiasm for your book(s).

2.a. Use Twitter to create a Friendship Circle.

Let's talk about how to derive maximum benefit from Twitter.

There are two circles at work in my system, and Twitter drives both. One is the Friendship Circle that gets you reviews and guaranteed buyers for future books. The other is the Viral Circle that attracts the attention of your target audience immediately, and gives your book sales a chance to soar overnight. We'll talk about the Viral Circle in 4.b.

Here's how it works:

I'm going to assume you already have a Twitter account and a few hundred followers (if you don't, ask anyone how to get a Twitter account and a few hundred followers. It will take you a week or two, at most).

Start following the live conversation threads, and/or the tweets of your followers. What you're looking for is a good friendship prospect. Eventually, it would be great if he or she chooses to help promote you someday. When you come across someone whose comments are interesting, click on their name and check their profile. If they have a website or blog, you've got a good prospect.

Click on their website and/or blog and start reading. Ask yourself if you feel this person has something of interest or value to offer your followers. Let's say @JaneSmith has written a blog this week about the people she helped at the burn center where she volunteers, and you found her words inspirational, and you decide she's the kind of friend you'd like to have.

Mention her in a tweet, recommending her to your followers.

Example: Jane, *@JaneSmith has written a blog about some very special people that touched my heart. Please* check it out: (insert the link to her blog).

Jane will see you have not only promoted her blog to all your followers, but that it meant something to you. She will publicly thank you. You will publicly respond, telling her how her blog made you *feel.* You are now in the early stage of what will probably become a close friendship.

Check her blog from time to time, and when she again writes something that moves you, or something you honestly feel will benefit your followers, mention it in another tweet. Over time, she will become a close friend and will probably follow your blog and read your books, and possibly recommend them to her followers.

This takes time. Lots of time. But every meaningful, worthwhile relationship takes time to build. It's important that you sincerely like Jane and consider her contributions valuable to the Twitter community. If not, it will show, and she and the Twitter community will think of you as a suck up, and you'll lose credibility.

2.b.　Drive your Twitter friends (and book readers) to your website.

Twitter is like being in junior high. You have two types of friends: those you see each day, and those you invite home for sleepovers. If you're using Twitter as a marketing tool, you MUST have a goal. And here it is: you have to get your friends to come to your house. If you don't get your Twitter pals onto your website, and into your email box, you may be making friends, which is great, but you're not marketing.

You need to have a goal for your Twitter involvement. And your goal has to be to get your Twitter pals OFF Twitter and onto your website, your blog, and into your email contacts list. If you're only interested in forming wonderful friendships, you can do that with Twitter by taking an active interest in what your friends are doing. But from a marketing standpoint it is almost NO BENEFIT to have 10,000 Twitter pals if you don't get some of them OFF Twitter and onto your promotional team.

2.c.   Drive them to your "Contact Me" button.

Drive your book readers to your website by putting a link at the beginning and end of your book. When they check out your website, make your "Contact Me" button easy to find.

Drive your Twitter friends to your website and blog site through your Twitter profile, your direct messages, and your email conversations. As soon as you know you've made a friend on Twitter, exchange emails. If someone hesitates to share their email, he or she is not a close friend yet.

2.d.   Personally email them.

This applies to people who read your books and leave comments on your website, as well as your Twitter friends who have shared their email address. My system requires you to personally respond to the emails you receive from your Twitter friends, blog friends, website friends, and anyone else who writes to you about your book.

2.e.   Convert them into loyal friends.

As you get to know these readers and Twitter folk, you will become close friends. The kind of friends who do things to help each other in the natural course of a friendship.

2.f.   Convert your loyal friends to buyers.

It's a natural progression for your closest Twitter pals to want to try at least one of your books. They will either like it or not. If they don't, they aren't likely to go out of their way to help promote you. But as your friend they will at the very least continue to re-tweet your good news and publicly thank you for promoting their work. And these things make a difference.

2.g.   Convert the buyers to reviewers.

If they *do* like your book, they might be willing to post a review on Amazon. If they post one, it will be a good review. My recommendation is not to ask for a review, which is very intimidating to most people, but to ask for a simple blurb.

> **Example:** Jane Smith emails me and says, "I loved *Wish List*! I started reading it at eight last night and couldn't put it down! I wound up reading the entire book in one sitting!"

It would be simple for me to say, "Is there any way I could talk you into just pasting those words into the Amazon Review box? It would mean the world to me!"

If she doesn't write me that type of email, I might ask for a blurb, which is usually just one or two sentences.

Blurbs are easier to ask for than reviews, easier to get, and what really counts is getting her to click that 5-star button.

2.h. Put them on your Guaranteed Buyer mailing list.

It takes a lot to get a Twitter person to this point. The Guaranteed Buyer List (GBL) is the ultimate goal of all your activity. When you get enough names on this list your next book is guaranteed to hit the best seller list!

The GBL is NOT just a list of people who ask to be notified about your next book. It's a list of people who have made these sorts of comments:

"I love your books. Please let me know when the next one is out. I will buy anything you write!"

"I would pay ten times the price you're charging. Please hurry up and write the next one!"

"I have recommended your books to everyone I know. I'm a fan for life!"

"Stop answering my emails and spend your time writing your next book! I crave the next Creed. Hurry!"

—People who make these types of comments are guaranteed buyers. My ultimate goal is to have 10,000 of them!

2.i. <u>Email them to promote your next book.</u>

Once you have people on your GBL you will notify them in an email about your next book. Because they are guaranteed buyers, they will buy your book immediately. You will send a few hundred of these emails every day, for as many days as you have names, and as they buy your book, the volume will build, and your book will start moving up the charts. When it hits the Top 100, it will be found by book buyers who are searching for new books based on several criteria: Movers and Shakers, Top 100, Top Books in a Certain Genre, Number of Positive Reviews, and/or Bargain Books, which generally means $2.99 and lower.

Assorted Comments About Twitter:

You can get two things out of Twitter that can change your life. One is friendship and the other is sales. I get both, and you can, too.

For me, the purpose of Twitter is to make friends, then convert them into a promotional team that will help you become successful. You do this by being a sincere, loyal friend, and by helping your Twitter friends become successful.

You can get what you want out of Twitter, but you don't get there by tweeting that you ate your burger without pickles today, or you slept in late, or you hate your boss. You don't get there by posting famous quotations. You don't get there by promoting your books.

What? What did I just say? You don't get there by promoting your *books*?

Let me explain. Yes, you can promote a little bit. A *very* little bit. But ONLY when you've achieved something special. For instance, if you just hit the 50,000 sales mark, that deserves a tweet. But you don't announce: "I just hit the 50,000 sales mark!" Instead, you say, "Thanks to my loyal Twitter friends, I just hit a huge milestone: 50,000 sales! I could not have achieved this without your help." That type of announcement sounds far less promotional and much more like gratitude.

Beyond special achievements, you should virtually never promote yourself on Twitter. Why? Because if you're working Twitter properly, your friends will promote you, and you can publicly respond to their comments, adding a little along the way.

> **Example:** Let's say Jane and I have become close friends and I never miss an opportunity to promote her work. I tell Jane my latest book has come out. She reads it and likes it. On her own, Jane will probably tweet something to all her followers like, "Check out John Locke's newest book, *Don't Poke the Bear!* @DonovanCreed. I loved it, and you will, too! Link: (XYZ)"

When Jane puts @DonovanCreed in her message it allows me to see it in my Twitter "mentions" box. This gives me a chance to publicly thank Jane for her tweet, and add a little promotion, if possible.

Example: "Thanks @JaneSmith for trying my Bear book! Thanks to you and my other great Twitter pals, *Don't Poke the Bear* just became a Kindle Best Seller!"

Some of your followers and some of Jane's will re-tweet your comment, because they're supportive people. When they do, any number from dozens to hundreds of people will see it, and some will be looking for a good book to read. When strangers re-tweet your comments, you'll thank them publicly, and start reading their blogs or tweets. If you feel they're good friend/promotional candidates, you repeat the process and start the whole Friendship Circle with them.

Again, never promote yourself, except in passing. Tweet about the people you like and the people who have written or done something you think your readers will find interesting. The key is to be sincere in your praise, and if you're referencing an article or blog post or website, be sure to give people a link they can click in the tweet that takes them straight to it.

A word about managing your Twitter followers: I "unfollow" anyone who uses the "bird" picture, anyone who is aggressively selling, anyone who isn't following me, and everyone who hasn't posted a tweet in the last three months. This gives you a solid list of followers who are more likely to appreciate the links you're sending out. When you get a mention like this, you know you're doing the right thing: "John, thanks for recommending @JaneSmith. I loved her blog, as I enjoy all your @DonovanCreed recommendations!"

If you do what I outlined above, you will quickly be overwhelmed by friends, and you'll be devoting lots of time to reading other people's posts and blogs, and there are only so many hours in the day. I always (eventually) answer those who mentioned me, then I have a list of my close Twitter friends, and I will mention as many as I can when I have the time. Sometimes I go weeks without tweeting, and sometimes I spend six hours tweeting about the blogs and posts I found interesting. My close Twitter friends know that when I send out 20 "praises" one after the other, I'm not being a phony. They know I've read those blogs and jotted down the info over several hours or days. They know this because we've built a rapport over time, and they know I often have to "go dark" (meaning I have to occasionally stop Twittering for awhile) when trying to catch up on my emails or writing.

I keep an off-line list of my closest Twitter friends, with links to their sites. I often create a shortened URL link so I'll have more characters available to write something nice about them. I use tinyurl.com, which shortens any URL to only 26 characters, and is free. I try to say something about my friends on a regular basis. By monitoring the off-line list, I can see if it's been awhile since I posted. If so, I paste the link to their blog or website into my search engine and check out what they've written lately. If I like it, I post. If they haven't posted anything new since my last tweet, I post something else that is applicable to their business or their character.

How much time should you devote to Twitter? Try for an hour each day. Just be sure not to get sucked in. I mean that in the nicest way, because Twitter is massively addicting! Try the hour a day plan and see what that does for you.

How many close friends do you need? I don't know. But I have around 100 close Twitter friends who have become email friends, and most of those are solid enough to put on my Guaranteed Buyer's List (GBL).

But even though the numbers aren't large, there are other benefits to doing all this. For example, I'm closer to these Twitter people than I am to most of the people I know "in real life!" —I can't stress this enough: don't be a phony. Only get to know people you admire and care for. Because Twitter is just too flippin' much work not to love the people you're dealing with!

Here's what I've learned that most people don't seem to know:

Twitter pals don't often buy books or give reviews, but Twitter email friends do both!

Sure, a few will buy your books and post reviews without being your email friend. But they're the exception. What you want to do is get these wonderful people off Twitter and onto your email list. Upgrade them from "pal" to "friend." This is why you're hand-picking people you like from the Twitter feeds! Since you personally chose them, you WILL be sincere! You want to cultivate these friendships. They will *want* to help you, because you've been helping *them*. They will help you even if they don't love your books. But if they *do* love your books, you will eventually get them on your GBL.

It takes a lot of time and effort to get Twitter people on your GBL, and *no* time and effort to get book readers on it! So why invest all that time and energy into Twitter? —Because you've got to get your book on one of the Kindle search lists, so strangers can find them. And that takes hundreds of sales and more than a dozen great reviews. And a great way to get those initial sales and reviews is through the effort you make with Twitter (and Facebook and other social media platforms).

To recap, I select people I'd like to have as friends because they're cool, smart, classy, interesting, and so forth. As we get to know each other publicly, I try to help them by driving traffic to their excellent websites and blog posts. As our friendship grows, they want to help me, too. But it's not like we're helping each other through obligation. We're helping each other the same way close friends do. If they're not interested in my help, or in helping me, we will remain public friends, because I still think they're special people. But those I can get onto my website, and blog site, and onto my email list, might become loyal book buyers. So it's a progression, just like any friendship. The only difference is, when I find someone I want to help, I'm hoping they will eventually want to help me, as well.

The more quality followers you have, the better you can help your Twitter friends. So you should keep building your follower list until *you* feel you have enough to do a good job for the people you're praising. In your mind that could be 500, or 50,000. As I've said, I keep mine at 20,000. If 20,000 people have a chance to read what I write about @JaneSmith, Jane will consider me a valuable resource.

When Jane sees me promoting her business, her books, or her blog to 20,000 people on a semi-regular basis, she will want to reciprocate, and will re-tweet positive posts about me to her followers, and will recommend my books, and possibly choose to post an Amazon review for me.

Twitter is a wonderful site, but you need to be pro-active. And everything I've said in this section applies not only to Twitter, but Facebook and all the other social media sites. But when we get to Section 4.b., I think that's where Twitter separates itself from all the other platforms.

I doubt you can make much money with your Twitter contacts if you don't develop a friendship OFF Twitter. And you can't make a fortune even if you do. But developing Twitter promotional partners should be part of your overall marketing plan. As I've said, when we get to Section 4.b. you will see the best possible use of Twitter for your marketing strategy.

3.   <u>Create a Simple, Non-Nonsense Blogsite</u>.

In the past I've used blogspot and wordpress, and both were fine. Now I'm posting directly to the home page of my website. The natural tendency people have when they're designing a blog site is to make it fancy. I recommend you keep it simple because what you want is their eyes on the content of your blog post, and nothing else, except that at the end of your post, they should be able to find links to purchase your books.

3.a. Post short, infrequent, *Loyalty Transfer* blogs to your Target Audience that showcase your writing ability and unique style. Make sure your reader has a link to your book(s) near the end of each blog post.

Everyone has a way of blogging that makes him or her unique. But few authors embrace the concept that LESS is MORE. You may post a blog every day, and perhaps all your subscribers read each daily post, but I doubt it. I think if you post every day most of your subscribers will delete them unread. I may be wrong, and hope I am. I'm not basing my opinion on anything more than a feeling about blogs in general, and you might be the exception. If you are, good for you.

My approach to blogging is to post approximately 12 to 15 blogs...per *year*!

That's not a misprint. I rarely write two blogs in the same month, and never write unless I have a specific purpose. I spend weeks deciding on the topic and days trying to determine the most effective way to present it, which will always amount to less than 800 words. I spend hours composing, formatting and shaping it into the best blog I can write.

Here's what's about to happen: in a few minutes you're going to read three of my sample blogs, and you're going to scratch your head and think, *what's the big deal?*

And that's a good thing.

I want people to think my blogs are off-the-cuff posts. It's not important that anyone knows how many hours I worked on them, or what the sum of my reasons were for writing them. But while we're on the subject, there are four reasons I write short, infrequent blogs:

I want a lot of subscribers, and I believe the best way to keep them happy is to NOT inundate them with content.

I want to prove to my loyal subscribers that I value their time.

I want my subscribers to be eager for my next post. I want them to be excited to find a new one in their email box. I've subscribed to blogs in the past only to be saturated with daily musings that often contain errors and poorly-thought topics that appear to be thrown at me for no other reason than to have something to say. After a few days of that, I tend to delete them as soon as they arrive.

I want to attract many more subscribers, and when people come to check out my blog posts they'll see how few I've written, how short they are, and hopefully, they'll like what I have to say, and will want to subscribe.

To recap: my goal in writing short, infrequent blogs is to attract and keep subscribers, and obtain 100% readership for each post.

My Blogs

There is a purpose for every blog I write, and that purpose is to make sales. Having said that, of course I write blogs I hope are entertaining, interesting, informative, and do justice to the subject. *Although I have a purpose, I'm not manipulating anyone, because I care deeply about the subjects and people I write about. When you write a book that comes from your heart, do you not hope people will buy that book? It's the same with my blogs. Except that my blogs come at people in a very subtle way.*

My blogs are designed to attract my target audience, and get them to try one of my books.

<u>Repeat</u>: my blogs are designed to attract my target audience!

<u>Repeat</u>: my blogs are designed to attract my target audience!

I very rarely come right out and ask them to try one of my books, and when I do, it's part of the theme of the blog, and not just a commercial.

I know my target audience, and I write the type of blog that attracts them in a subtle way. Remember what I wrote earlier about my target audience? They love everyday heroes. They're compassionate, but are drawn to the outrageous, and have a dry sense of humor. They're busy people who are frazzled and stressed out and seeking stress relief. They love a quiet hero who lets his actions speak for him, which means he's usually underappreciated. They like a plot twist and the idea that the hero doesn't understand women, and makes his bewilderment plausible to the reader without coming across as whining. They know I don't take myself seriously as a writer and don't expect them to take me seriously, either. They know the sole purpose of my writing is to make them smile or laugh for a few hours on a day when they need it most.

I write blogs that are universal and timeless. Universal in order to attract a wide audience, and timeless to let them "stew" like you'd put a spaghetti sauce in the refrigerator so the flavors will have time to come together better. Only I intend my blogs to spark interest months and years from now. I believe the things I write will be EVEN MORE APPLICABLE months and years from now.

I write my blogs in the same style I write my books. When you write a purposeful blog, you should come up with subjects and stories that cater to the emotions of your target audience, while showcasing your writing ability and unique style.

Example #1:

This one is simple. It's the first blog I wrote. When I designed my marketing system I knew my personal blog would play a huge part. Unfortunately, I had never blogged before, so the first thing I had to do was create a blog site!

I titled this post *The Shopping Cart*, and it's a story about something silly that actually happened to me. It could have been written many ways, but I chose to write it directly to my target audience. As you read it, pay attention to the thematic elements: the everyday, quiet, unappreciated hero, the dry humor, the weird situation, the odd dialogue, the plot twist, and the idea that the hero doesn't understand women, doesn't impress the girl, and makes his bewilderment plausible to the reader without coming across as whining. All these thematic elements can be found in my books. When I drive you to my blog, and you read this little story, there will be a link in the right margin where you can click on one of my books, or view a book trailer. From there you're one step away from buying a book. Notice also, I'm letting the reader know Donovan Creed is a hero, a book character, and that I write books. I'm *not* asking the reader to buy my books. But I *am* pitching the book-buying message through a story.

Again, you might read this silly little story and think, *big deal!* But I can tell you it strikes a subtle chord in my target audience. If it doesn't strike a subtle chord in you, you're probably not part of my target audience. It's not meant to be a moment like, *Oh my God, this is so well written I want to buy this guy's books right now!*

It's more like, *Cool. This guy writes books? I wonder what they're like (click).*

Don't get hung up on Example #1. It was a first step. Examples #2 and #3 are giant steps. How giant? Example #2 turned me into a best-selling author overnight! Example #3 will eventually add hundreds of names to my GBL! So just because this first example is minimal, don't give up on me. I'm starting with this one to show you the progression of how I use thematic elements in my blogs and to prove I have a plan for every blog I write. And that plan is to attract an audience and get them to click on one of my books in the right-hand margin of the page. And it works.

The Shopping Cart
Posted on <u>October 25, 2010</u> by <u>jplocke</u>

My new business cards were delivered on Friday, the ones that have a photograph of my book covers on the front, with the words, "A Donovan Creed Novel." I kept forgetting to carry them Saturday, but yesterday I put one in my pocket.

Yesterday was a windy day with occasional sudden gusts. Though it was warm, the leaves were falling – a definite sign autumn was upon us, so I decided to make a couple of loafs of pumpkin bread. I drove to Kroger's, got the ingredients and a few other items. After unloading my cart, I carefully put it in the cart rack, making sure the wind wouldn't dislodge it, or the other carts in the rack, then headed back to my car. A sudden gust of wind hit, and I instinctively looked over at the cart rack. Those carts were fine, but I saw another one in the distance that was flying across the lot, heading right for a lady who was unloading groceries into the trunk of her car. She didn't see the cart coming, had no idea she was about to take a high-velocity hit from a runaway shopping cart.

I yelled, "Watch out!" and pointed to the cart.

She turned to look at me, but not the cart. I started running right at her, and she froze. I raced twenty yards or so while pointing at the cart. She finally looked at it and her face blanched. I hurled myself at the cart and managed to stop it only inches before impact.

She snapped, "You think that's funny?"

I shrugged. "I thought it was heroic."

"They should put you in prison," she said, then finished loading her groceries and drove away.

Now I'm in the Subway Restaurant, ordering lunch to take home. Figure I'll eat before starting the pumpkin bread. There's a guy and girl working the counter. I place my order. Suddenly the guy sees something outside the window and takes off running. The girl and I watch him fly across the parking lot. He grabs a runaway cart just before it crashes into a lady's car. She's so appreciative she hugs him.

The girl at the counter gushes, "He's like that."

"Like what?" I say.

"He's like a hero. You know, the way he dashes off and helps people."

"Well," I said. "The world needs heroes."

"It does," she said. "Too bad there aren't many out there."

"Oh, they're out there," I said. "You just don't always see them."

She thought a minute. "You mean like Batman?"

"Yeah," I said. "Like Batman. And..."

She arched her brows. "And?"

"And Donovan Creed."

"Donovan Creed?" she said. "Who's that?"

I reached into my pocket and handed her my card.

If I were writing a daily blog, without a specific purpose, and this incident happened today, my blog post might look like this:

Funny thing happened today. A runaway shopping cart nearly hit a woman in a Kroger parking lot. I intercepted it and she yelled at me! Go figure! Has anything like this ever happened to you? Please share!

This is similar to tons of blog posts I've read, but there's no way it's going to sell eBooks. You can tell that, right? So if this is what you're doing, then yes, you're engaging your subscribers, but you're not generating any sales activity!

By the way, the first three days after I wrote *The Shopping Cart* I sold more books than I did during the entire month of September.

Example #2:

This is the blog that changed my life. You may read it and say, "I don't get it." That's fine. But this blog generated more than 5,000 views in two days and went viral. People sent it all over the world. The link was posted on chat sites all over the country. During the four weeks after posting this blog, I sold 1,300 eBooks, which is more sales than I made the previous seven months, combined! As those 1,300 people bought my other books and spread the word, my sales grew exponentially. The following month, December, I sold 13,681 eBooks! And of course as those people told their friends and bought my other books, sales continued to grow.

You can have the world's greatest book, but if you can't find a way to get it in front of an audience, nothing else matters.

This blog is titled, *Why I Love Joe Paterno and My Mom!* It's only 550 words long, but it's 550 words that changed my life!

Why I Love Joe Paterno and my Mom!
Posted on November 3, 2010 by jplocke

I am not a Penn State grad.

I have never attended Penn State University.

I have never done business with Joe Paterno or Penn State in any fashion.

But I love the man.

115

Have, in fact, loved him for 44 years.

My father died when I was two, and my mom had no interest in re-marrying because, as she put it, "I'm already married!" She pro-vided for my brother and me, working hard to ensure we had eve-rything we needed.

And she gave us bonus love.

When I was a teenager, singing in a rock and roll band, my mom was concerned about the lack of male influence in my life. She told me to find a role model, someone I could look up to. She said to pick that person, but choose wisely. She said, "Choose a person of high character. If you do, he will never let you down." She said, "Watch how he handles adversity and success, and emulate his be-havior." She also said, "If it turns out you made the wrong choice, you can learn from that, too."

About that time I read an article in a magazine about a young coach at Penn State who had an idea for a "grand experiment." He wanted to coach kids to be student athletes. He vowed to run a clean program, and promised to take a personal interest in his ath-letes' academic life. He wanted to graduate — not football players — but citizens of the world.

I began following Joe, and over the years gained enormous respect for the life lessons he taught. Joe reinforced the lessons I'd learned from my mother about integrity, loyalty, generosity, commitment, and others. I highlighted many of those lessons in a book I wrote 30 years ago, "Qualities of Character."

Over the years I watched Joe experience success and setbacks, and my mom was right, he never let me down. Joe is still coaching, fei-sty as ever, and still runs a squeaky-clean program and continues, year after year, to have one of the highest athlete graduation rates in the nation. He has personally donated more than $5 million to Penn State, and together with his wife, Sue, Joe has procured – get this – $1 BILLION in donations to his beloved university!

When I finally got a chance to meet Joe in person, I told him how he had positively impacted my life. I said, "In fact, you're the second best role model a guy could have."

He said, "Who's the best?"

"My mom."

"I'd like to meet her," he said.

"She's a hard core Red Sox fan," I warned.

"I'm a Brooklyn Dodgers fan," he said.

"Brooklyn?"

He laughed. "They shoulda stayed in Brooklyn."

–Joe could probably tell you the last day the Dodgers played in Brooklyn: September 24, 1957, when they beat Pittsburgh 2-0.

"They shoulda stayed"? –Well, maybe so. Joe had tons of offers to coach elsewhere for more money. But he stayed at Penn State all these years anyway. He remained faithful to his school, just as my mom remained faithful to her deceased husband.

They say it takes all kinds to make a world, but I can't help thinking what a much better world it would be if there were more people in it like Joe Paterno and my mom.

That blog is only 550 words long, but it took me two full days to write. To give you an idea how carefully I wrote it, consider that I can write 7,000 words a day when I'm writing novels.

Let's talk about the thematic elements in this blog that are found in my books:

The style of writing
A heroic individual
An intelligent, independent, strong woman
Humor
Loyalty
Generosity
Respect

There are two main reasons this blog worked. The first is, the people who admire Joe Paterno, and the people who admire wonderful mothers liked my style of writing. The second is, I utilized for the first time my new invention, what I call *Loyalty Transfer*.

After writing this post I tweeted the title and link to my followers several times throughout the day, and many of my closest Twitter friends re-tweeted it to all their followers. Then I went one step further (this is the Viral Circle I mentioned earlier). I posted the link on Twitter with hash tags for Joe Paterno. Then I ran a Twitter search for Penn State and found hundreds of people tweeting to each other about the upcoming game against Northwestern. I picked the first 100, knowing most of them would still be online at the time, and sent each one of them an individual tweet with the title of my blog and a link to it. Based on the title alone, most, if not all of them clicked the link and read my blog post. Then they began forwarding it to friends all over the world. It wound up being posted on Penn State's official website and was the highlighted blog of the day.

And I started selling books like crazy!

Loyalty Transfer means, this blog appealed to Joe Paterno fans and fans of wonderful mothers. Those people appreciated what I wrote, and the way I wrote it. The result? They felt a kinship to me through my blog, and transferred their loyalty from Joe and great moms to me, a total stranger. They clicked my books. Many enjoyed them and bought more, enjoyed those, and recommended them to their friends.

And the momentum continued to build!

Okay, so this is a universal, timeless blog. What I mean by that is it will be just as fresh this year as it was last year. If Joe Paterno retires in a year or in ten years, this blog could become even more popular. In other words, when football season starts in September of this year, I can pick another 100 Penn State fans and send them the link again! When Joe retires I can send the link again. This blog should be timeless. It should be relevant for as long as people fondly remember Joe Paterno and/or their mothers!

<u>Example #3:</u>

This blog is titled, *Michael J. Fox and your Loved Ones!* It's another example of a universal, timeless blog that will work a year from now, five years from now, and could become more relevant as time goes on. My first three blogs were written days apart, because I was fine-tuning. But when I wrote the Joe Paterno blog, I wrote nothing else for nearly five months! For almost five months, that is the blog post you saw when I drove you to my blog site. I let it sit there all that time, influencing more and more people.

If I wrote a different blog post every day, or every week, my Joe Paterno blog would not have had much impact. It would be buried it under a hundred blogs by now. Seriously, how many people are going to subscribe to your blog and dig through hundreds of previous posts?

Less is more!

I've been blogging since October, 2010. If you check my blog posts you will see I have written a grand total of...seven blogs! And all seven are just as relevant today as they were when I wrote them, and all will be relevant years from now.

I try to keep my blogs under 600 words. My longest was 806 words, and that one helped propel *Follow the Stone*, a *western*, all the way to #34 on the Amazon/Kindle Best Seller List, and helped it remain on the list for 71 days!

Here's the Michael J. Fox blog. As you read it, see if you can find the thematic elements that "speak" to my target audience. I bet you're getting the hang of it now!

Michael J. Fox and Your Loved Ones

Posted on April 12, 2011 by jplocke

I've never met Michael J. Fox, and doubt I ever will. He's not a fan so far as I know, and has almost certainly never heard of me. I'm not seeking his endorsement. This is a tiny blog with a very small readership, so he'll never read these words.

In short, there's nothing in it for me...to write about him. Which is proof these words come from my heart.

I'll make this short. As you know, I value your time, and only write when I feel I have something important to say. I could wait till Mike is in the news, but that would be opportunistic, and unworthy of the subject matter.

I'm busy, you're busy. But I'm pausing a moment to express my admiration and gratitude for not only Mike, who is an extraordinary human being, but for all those special people who exude character and class every day of their lives while fighting debilitating diseases hell-bent on breaking them down and killing their spirits. I'm talking about not only Mike, but your friends and mine, and our relatives.

I'm sure Mike has rough days where he struggles to stay positive, days when fatigue gets the better of him, days when he wonders from what reservoir can he possibly extract another ounce of strength. But here's a guy...wow! I'm almost at a loss for words. It takes a lot of courage for a former leading man to put himself out there and take his battle to the enemy in front of all the world's cameras. So truly...wow!

And yet, we all have friends and relatives who have it even worse than Mike. These quiet family heroes bravely battle incurable diseases without the benefit of an adoring public. My cousin, Susan's, battle would overwhelm me in no time, and yet she maintains an attitude that shames me to complain about the insignificant trials I face. I have a friend, Lisa, who's in the middle of a tragic battle. She's showing us all, by example, what it means to have true courage. Your friends and relatives are doing the same. I wish I could single each of them out and praise their epic, individual examples.

Mike, Susan, Lisa...and your friends and family members are giving us a blueprint for how to live our lives with courage and dignity. They're teaching us how to face fear and overcome obstacles. How to live extraordinary lives in the face of crushing physical and emotional devastation.

I only know Michael J. Fox through his TV and movie roles and public appearances, and I don't know your loved ones at all. But I love them. Love them the same way I love my friends and family members who bravely fight the fight. Love their mental toughness. Admire their ability to handle adversity.

I write books about kooky characters and larger-than-life heroes, but I'll tell you something right now: the amazing true-life heroes we all know and love are everything that's right, noble and true about humankind. Their remarkable determination, unbreakable will, and their indomitable courage will surely be placed as credits to their names in Paradise.

Michael J. Fox is the name of this blog, and its face. But it's a blog about all who struggle daily, while displaying the mental fortitude to prevail against overwhelming odds. It's for all the Dick Clarks of the world. The Roger Eberts. The Susans, the Lisas, and it's for your parents, your siblings, your friends and your loved ones. So when I say Mike, I'm talking about a million amazing people who are absolutely worth pausing a few minutes to think about and honor. Since I can't single everyone out by name, I'll just say:

Keep fighting the good fight, Mike. I love you, man!

Did you catch the thematic elements? And the subtle way I referenced I'm an author who writes about "larger-than-life heroes?" Are you beginning to see why I spend a month thinking about the best possible blog I can write, and why I spend countless hours paring it down to a short, powerful testimonial to people of courage and everyday heroes? Don't forget, when you go to my website, www.donovancreed.com, the first thing you see is my most recent blog. And it will sit there for at least a full month, attracting readers for my books. At the top of the page you'll see photos of the covers of my book. Along the right margin you'll see video book trailers and links to my books. The links to my books are conveniently located near the bottom of the blog. If I write a blog of more than 800 words, you would have to scroll up to click on the book links, which is yet another reason I keep the blogs short!

This blog, like the others, is timeless. Whenever Michael J. Fox is back in the news, I could go on Twitter, find a dozen people talking about Mike, or Parkinson's, and send them the link. I also post hash tags when notifying my Twitter pals about my latest blogs. I also tag my blogs with all the appropriate key words, so it will show up in search engines when words like "Joe Paterno" and "Penn State" and "Michael J. Fox" and Parkinson's Disease" are typed.

My blogs are written with a specific purpose, and that is to show people how I write, what types of books I write, and to inspire them to take action and click on my books through *Loyalty Transfer*, and to constantly reinforce the themes that appeal to the hero in all of us that is not always appreciated by the masses.

This is not a case of manipulation. It's a case of me writing from the heart, about things I believe in deeply. These themes and the way I write them "speak" to my target audience, and make them want to read my books.

4.   Promote Your Blog

You'll want to provide a link to your blog at the end of your books. Also, if your blog is separate from your website, you should reference it in all the emails you send to new people. The most important list you can build is Guaranteed Buyers, but right behind that is your list of Blog Subscribers. So book links are one way to promote your blog, your emails another, and Twitter is yet a third way.

4.a.   Use Twitter to generate buzz and create leads.

You've got two types of Twitter followers: pals and friends. Twitter pals are the ones you chat with, and have fun with online. Twitter friends are the ones you know well enough to exchange emails with and help. When I've posted a new blog, I write a couple of general tweets to my 20,000 followers and hope some will visit my blog and re-tweet the link. I also send group tweets to Twitter pals, maybe four to six pals per message, and maybe six to ten tweets altogether, so I've hit around forty pals. I also send individual tweets to some of my close Twitter friends to tell them about the blog. They always re-tweet the news, often with a personal endorsement. I'll send those to about six to ten close friends, and scatter these tweets over the course of a couple of days, at different times. I don't hit *all* my friends and pals for each blog, just enough of them to create buzz. I tweet to different friends each time so I'm not hassling the same people every month. When they re-tweet my news, I let a few hours go by, or maybe a day, and then re-tweet their "re-tweets," spreading the messages out so I'm hitting different times of the day and night. This keeps the buzz going.

4.b.   Use Twitter search and hash tags to create a Viral Circle.

In addition to the tags you use when publishing your blog post, this step can help you go viral. Using my Michael J. Fox blog as an example, when I send a general tweet to my followers to announce the blog post, I might use a hash tag #Michael J. Fox in one, and #Parkinson's in another. This creates or copies a Twitter category that gives your link a chance to be seen by anyone who seeks those categories. Also, I might conduct a Twitter search for Michael J. Fox and another for Parkinson's, and there might be a dozen people tweeting about one or both of those subjects. For example, let's say @Martha has tweeted about seeing Mike on the Ellen show. I'll respond to her tweet with a comment, and maybe re-tweet her message. If she follows me and responds to thank me, I might send her an individual tweet: "@Martha if you get a chance, check out *Michael J. Fox and*

Your Loved Ones: (link)." I'll repeat the process with several or many of the people on that category list, over time. If there are a dozen, I'll meet and become friends with the whole dozen and send them individual invitations to view the link. I became friends with 100 people I met through the category search for Penn State after writing the Joe Paterno blog that changed my life. You could repeat this process every few weeks or months if you followed my system, because you will have written timeless, universal blogs, and you're making friends with people who share your common interest. The friends you meet through common interests will enrich your life.

Let me explain what you're trying to do. It's one thing to build a list of 5,000 Twitter followers. Quite another to populate that list with 5,000 people who share your interests! So if I love dogs and write a post about my dog, I might do a Twitter Search for "dog lovers." Hundreds will show up. I will start following these people, re-tweet their posts, and engage them in conversation. As they follow me, I am building the type of Twitter followers who will respond to my blog posts. As I get comfortable with them, I invite them to view my blog post. Because I keep my post current for at least 30 days, I've got that much time to bond with these people, but usually it only takes a few minutes or hours to make a solid connection, because they were Tweeting live when I found them, and because we have a shared interest.

The reason this is so valuable is because you're becoming friends with Twitter people who are very loyal to your subject matter, whether it's comic books, authors, moms, or whatever your theme or subject matter is. You're not selling them anything, you're simply meeting them through a common interest, populating your Twitter follower list with like-minded friends, and recommending they check out your latest blog. It's very low key. If they read your blog and like it, they might leave a comment and/or click your book link. They may also re-tweet your blog link to their friends or others with whom they share a common interest related to your subject.

As I said, I met 100 people and sent them a personal invitation to view my Joe Paterno post, and within twenty-four hours more than 5,000 people showed up! I noticed an immediate impact on my book sales, which continued to grow exponentially, because many who purchased my books liked them enough to buy the whole series!

4.c. Drive your Twitter friends (and book readers) to your blog site.

I covered this in 4.a., but made it a separate step for the outline.

4.d. Convert the viewers to blog subscribers.

You need to display, very prominently, a place for your viewers to become blog subscribers. Again, it helps if your subscribers know you're going to blog infrequently, and that your blogs are short and interesting. Your subscribers will often become OOU's because if they continue reading your blogs it's because they like your style. If they like your style, they almost certainly like your writing.

4.e. <u>Convert the subscribers to loyal friends, book buyers and review writers</u>.

This is the natural result of the friendships you build over time through email conversations with your blog subscribers, book readers, Twitter friends, and so forth. You're helping your friends; they're helping you.

4.f. <u>Put them on your Guaranteed Buyer mailing list</u>.

This should be the ultimate goal of all your activity. There is nothing more valuable to you than your GBL, your Guaranteed Buyer List. This is the list of your super fans. They're the key to your future as an author. If an author can get 10,000 people on this type of list, he or she could rule the world!

4.g.   Email them to promote your next book.

Don't badger the people on this list! Email them only when you have a new product. Send them a short email (less than a full page) to catch them up on any awards you've received, achievements you've hit *because of them*! And tell them about your new book and include a link so they can click on it before returning to their email program. I always put at least two purchase links in the message, sometimes three, in case they don't want to read the whole thing! I make the announcement there's a new book available, then put in a link. The next couple of paragraphs tell them what's happened since my last notification, then a link. The next paragraph tells them why they might enjoy the new book, then a link. Then I thank them for their loyalty, and that's it.

I send up to 250 of these a day to the people on my GBL. These are loyal fans, and they will spread the message on blog boards, conversation threads, and by emailing their friends and family members. Those 250 will each influence at least ten friends and relatives. The next day I'll send out another 250, and continue sending 250 a day until I'm out of names!

Once your book gets into the Top 100, there are many ways for total strangers to find you, as I've mentioned previously: Movers and Shakers, Top 100, Top Books in a Certain Genre, Number of Positive Reviews, and/or Bargain Books, which generally means $2.99 and lower.

5.   ePublish Your Book.

If you have more time on your hands than cash in your pocket, and if you're a do-it-yourself type of person, you can save a lot of money by *literally* self-publishing your books, personally handling every phase of the project. Don't let anyone kid you, it's a lot of work. By the same token, don't let anyone tell you it's too difficult. If you do it yourself, you'll surely make some mistakes along the way. But the mistakes you make will only delay you, not destroy you! So this is something you can do, if you're determined.

Or you can take a partnership approach with a services provider, whereby you do the things you're comfortable doing, and pay the provider to do the rest.

Or you can do what I do: pay someone else to deal with it. I'm fortunate to be in a position where my time and stress is more precious to me than the cash it requires to turn the whole publishing project over to a company that specializes in offering a turn-key solution to ePublishing.

I don't want this next part to sound like a commercial, so I'm not going to recommend a particular company. I happen to use Telemachus Press, but I know there are plenty of companies in the business, and if I were you I'd do an internet search and talk to several different providers before making a decision. Again, this is a decision you should make after contacting several provider companies. Regardless of who you use, it's not cheap. But if you can afford it, you will have that much more time available to write books and answer emails!

5.a. Use Social Media to generate buzz and leads and drive traffic to your website and blog site so you can continue fueling the Friendship Circle.

We have covered this several times, and it's part of the cycle. To recap, you create buzz on Facebook, Twitter, and any other social platforms you may use, in order to drive traffic to your website, in order to get people to click on your Contact button, so you can get a feel for their interest level. Now that you have their email addresses, you can begin developing friendships that might eventually turn them into Guaranteed Buyers!

You put links in your books that take readers directly to your website for the same reason: to get your readers off your book and onto your website so they can click your Contact button. And the cycle continues.

You also create social media buzz in order to drive traffic to your BLOG so you can get them to click on your book, so they will buy it, read it, and click on the link to your website, so they can click on your Contact button, and so on.

6. Repeat the Cycle with Future Books.

This step is obvious, and shouldn't require further explanation.

How to Write a Life-Changing Blog

I CAN'T WRITE a life-changing blog for each of you, but I can show you how to write one. It's not a matter of writing a touchy-feely post. It's a matter of writing the type of post that "speaks" to your target audience, and bonds you to them by creating a *Loyalty Transfer*. The loyalty that already exists between your readers and your subject matter will transfer to you through the power of your blog. This works because your reader will feel an instant rapport, a *kinship* with you because of what you shared or revealed about yourself in the blog. This revelation creates an emotional connection between you and your reader, through the subject or theme of your blog.

Write your blog, and then find people to read it. You find them by making Twitter announcements about your blog, and especially by running a Twitter search by key words and/or subject matter. These specific readers are already sold on the subject or theme of your blog, and when you send them a tweet with a link to your blog there's a high probability they'll click on it. Almost from the moment they start reading your blog, they'll realize you are OOT (one of them). By the time they finish reading it, you will have formed a bond. As their eyes notice the margin on the right side of the page, they'll find a link to your book. They'll click and order it. Since they already like your writing style, they are pre-sold, and will give your book every possible chance. If your book captivates them, they'll share the experience with others.

The two paragraphs I just wrote are the essence of how I became a best-selling author. People might insist my success was due to nothing more than my pricing, but I had these same titles priced as hard and soft cover books for five months, and sold virtually nothing. Then I sold them as eBooks and priced them at 99 cents for seven months, and still sold virtually nothing. People might say it was the Christmas rush, but I experienced an 823% increase in sales in *November*! People might say my success was due to the quality of my writing. If it was, you're in luck, because you probably write better than I do! But again, the eBooks that showed an 823% increase in November are the same ones that sold almost nothing the first seven months they were available, so the quality of my writing hadn't changed.

While I believe all these things had a hand in my success (low price, Christmas rush, quality of writing), I didn't begin to experience *real* success until the first days after implementing my marketing system. I credit (1) my business approach to marketing my books, (2) my understanding of how to maximize the power of my books, (3) my website, (4) Twitter, and (5) my personal blog. Even now, whenever I write a blog, my sales show a marked increase the following week. It's not easy writing these types of blogs, but they're well worth the effort.

So how do you decide what to write and how to write it?

Suppose you've written a light-hearted book about a girl fresh out of college who lands a job at a high-powered fashion magazine, who has the added baggage of a giant dog and an unemployed boyfriend. Would you write a blog about quiet heroes, great mothers, Joe Paterno, or Michael J. Fox? Of course not! You'd write a humorous, personal, dialogue-driven blog that relates to the largely female audience between the ages of 18 and 45 who have experienced something similar. And by "similar" I don't mean a big-city magazine job. I mean an unemployed boyfriend, a demanding job, a crazy dog, a nightmare boss! You might throw in a couple of mild sexual references, if they're humorous and relate to the types of situations they'll find in your books. Think: *Sex in the City* meets *Devil Wears Prada*.

> **KEY:** Your blog must include a personal element, such as a story or revelation your readers can relate to. Otherwise they can't transfer their feelings about the subject or theme of your blog to you!

> **KEY:** I always talk about my OOU's. As I've said, OOU means, "One of Us." These are my most loyal readers, and I try to give them not just recognition, but the chance to feel a part of something special. And that

something varies from person to person, except that they all understand we're in this writing adventure together, as partners and friends, and we both have a responsibility for making it work. The OOU's are the front line of my army. They go out and spread the word. They write reviews. They write blogs. They defend me when others put me down. How could I not love them? They're amazing! Truly amazing! So anyway, the key to writing a life-changing blog is not to find popular people and write about them and hope there's a transfer of loyalty from them to your writing. The key is to show your readers that you are one of them.

For example, if my words about Joe Paterno are sincere (and everyone who knows me, knows they are!) then others who love the man will FEEL my sincerity, and we will have a bonding experience over the fact that Coach Paterno influenced my life. And because of that bonding experience, their loyalty for Joe will transfer to me, and they will feel a kinship with me, based on something we have in common, our mutual admiration for JoePa.

Could this idea be used to manipulate people? Yes, I expect it could. And I can think of nothing that would make me feel worse than to see you go in that direction. It would be like giving you a super power and watching you use it for evil. So please, stick to people and subjects you feel deeply about. Be honest, forthright and true. If that sounds hokey to you, I'm sorry you bought this book.

I don't even want to consider that possibility, because all the writers I've met on Twitter and elsewhere are wonderful people with kind hearts. So let's get back on subject. How do you write a life changing blog?

Start by figuring out who your target audience is, and what they want from your book.

I'm going to show you how I do this, step by step, by showing you how I handled a very tough assignment. I wrote a western book, then wanted to write a blog to build the audience for it. This time I followed my system and decided who my target audience was BEFORE I wrote the book. That made the assignment *much* easier. Still, this was a difficult blog to compose, and here's why:

1.   People in today's world don't want to read westerns. Getting the average Kindle reader to purchase a western novel is about as hard as getting a literary agent to read an unsolicited manuscript from an unknown author!

2.   Westerns have a stigma among the reading public. They're not flashy. They're not just low-tech, they're NO-tech, and remind people of their grandparents!

3.   There's only so much you can do with a western. You've got a man, a gun, a horse, and the woman he loves. Dusty towns, saloons, cowboys, Indians,

railroad trains, outlaws, gun play — this is what people think of when they hear the word "western."

4.   There is certainly an audience for westerns, and they're easy to locate. Unfortunately, that audience is extremely small. Your book could be #2,000 on Kindle and still be the #1 western.

5.   My biggest challenge was the gamble I took writing a genre-changing book, which means I couldn't even count on the small, but loyal, western audience! By creating an outrageous western with zany characters and situations, I knew going in I might alienate the existing fan base for westerns! By the same token, I felt my book was too low key and low tech for most Donovan Creed fans. In short, I had NO existing audience, other than the crossover I hoped to attract from my Creed fans. But I'd already been told my Creed fans do not, I repeat, DO NOT read westerns!

6.   I had to create a blog that would attract a whole new audience in addition to the few existing readers of Creed books and westerns I hoped to gain.

I don't know what your book is about, but I doubt you'll face a tougher writing assignment than the blog I intended to write to attract thousands of readers for my western novel, *Follow the Stone.*

The experts told me not to write a western in the first place, so I didn't ask their opinions on how to market it. I wouldn't have asked anyway, because by the time I wrote *Follow the Stone*, I had mastered my marketing system. But if those experts *had* advised me, they would have told me to make an announcement on Twitter, Facebook and other social media sites. They would tell me to get some reviews posted for it. They would tell me to announce it on my website and blog. They would tell me to do interviews and guest blogs to "get the word out."

These are actually all good ideas, but in many cases the results are like preaching to the choir. Yes, you'll get some scattered sales by doing these things. But you would have gotten most or all of these sales anyway, during the course of following my system. But here's the problem: after getting those dozens of sales, you'll go back to your experts and ask, "Now what?" And they'll point you to things that cost money: publicists, ads, press releases. And in my experience, these methods don't work for self-published authors.

Don't get me wrong. You want those dozens of sales. But there's so much left on the table if you're only using your blog and Twitter account to make announcements. You don't get a whole new segment of book buyers by sending out press releases or making announcements to the people who already know you. You get them by target marketing. By writing a *Loyalty Transfer* blog aimed at the group of people for whom you wrote the book in the first place. In the case of my western, that means moms and dads.

You're probably wondering what famous person I chose to write about. Who did you come up with, John Wayne?

The answer is I didn't write about any famous person.

A *Loyalty Transfer* blog doesn't need to be about famous people. In fact, the best blogs are *not* about others. They're about *you*, and how a subject or theme makes you *feel*. People need to know something about you, in order to form a bond, or kinship. With that in mind, here was my thought process as I tackled the job of writing this very difficult blog:

I started by asking myself, "*What's my goal?*"

I answered, "*Motivating people to click on the link to buy my book.*"

What questions might they want addressed or answered in my blog? "*How about why I wrote the book in the first place? And what's in it for them?*"

What personal experience can I share to form a bond, and what is the emotional connection? "*How about nostalgia? I'm an older guy, so nostalgia is easy.*"

But I don't want my blog to appeal exclusively to people my own age! I can go from age 18 to 100 for these westerns, but I decided my target audience would be moms and dads. I knew I'd get some Creed crossover, and some readers of westerns, too. So I wanted nostalgia to be in there, but I had to be careful how I presented it. The moms and dads I was looking for are in their thirties and forties. I didn't want to come across like Wilfred Brimley hawking Quaker Oats!

I spent a couple of days thinking about it, and remembered when I was a kid my friends and I went through a period of years where we loved our comic books. My favorite comic book was *Kid Colt, Outlaw*. I figured I would start the blog by explaining how those comics made me *feel*. Since nostalgia is an emotion, I didn't have to make these thirty and forty-year-old moms and dads connect to my actual comic book collection. I could use that example to strike a chord about the things that are important to us in our youth. Things like childhood books and toys. More importantly, I could make an emotional appeal to them, as a parent, about a universal parenting experience — like how we can help our kids get the most from their childhood years.

I wasn't there yet, but this is how my mind was working. So I kept thinking about my target audience. When you focus on them, and what motivates them, you can't go wrong. I wondered about the moms and dads who grew up in an age far removed from the western adventure comic books and TV shows. I was thinking about a nostalgic emotional appeal, but realized if all I'm talking about is my old comic books I'm going to come across as the world's most boring geezer!

Days passed. Then it hit me.

There's a common element to what I was thinking about, and that element is childhood. A childhood is something we all had, and something everyone in my age demographic has lost. And when we lost that childhood, what is it we lost?

Our wide-eyed wonder. Our innocence.

So that's the answer. I would write a blog about me and my *Kid Colt* comic books, and how I lost my childhood innocence. I would appeal to the moms and dads by showing them how we, as parents, can protect our own children, and why it's important that we help our kids hang onto their innocence as long as possible.

What does this have to do with westerns?

Why, it has *everything* to do with westerns, if I frame the emotions properly! If I can make you equate your youth with my books — for at least thirty seconds — you might click on the link to my book in the right-hand margin of the page. I'm hoping you'll understand that by clicking the link you're OOU, one of us. One who loves childhood laughter and smiles, and one who understands how precious those years were to us then, and are to our children now. And you and I realize that while this special time has been lost forever, it can be recaptured by reading something that was written specifically for this emotional connection to your past. Think: Peter Pan for adults!

See how nutty I am? Wouldn't you hate to live in MY brain? But the trick is, I really believe it! I wrote *Follow the Stone* so people could escape into a different, simpler world, and smile at the things I took so seriously in my childhood. Even though I created outrageous characters and situations in my novel, I remained true to the basic thematic elements of what westerns used to be, while demonstrating what a new, hip western *can* be. I wanted to breathe new life into an old, worn-out genre.

By this point I knew what I would write, but it took days to fine-tune and edit the words so the blog would end at the proper place for them to click on the link.

Note: when you go to my blog and check the responses, you'll see I did strike the emotional chord in my target audience I worked so hard to hit. You'll also see by reading my various blogs that I don't get lots of written responses. *The Shopping Cart* started the ball rolling, but only garnered 8 comments! *Why I Love Joe Paterno and My Mom* changed my life, but only attracted 11 comments! *Michael J. Fox and Your Loved Ones* only generated 25. And this one, *The Day I Lost My Innocence*, only received 30 comments.

Any idea why I receive so few written responses to these blogs, even though they remain active for weeks and sometimes months? The answer is simple: the people who read them don't have *time* to write a written response—they're too busy ordering my books! ☺

Okay, I've explained how I do it, and you ought to be able to follow my thought process and write an effective blog to attract an audience for your books. Here's what I wrote:

The Day I Lost My Innocence
Posted on <u>March 22, 2011</u> by <u>jplocke</u>

I was twelve years old, excited, knowing Pak-a-Sak had the new comic books on display.

I'd outgrown *Archie*, *Richie Rich*, *Donald Duck* and *Casper* years earlier; and very recently and reluctantly, *Superman*, *Incredible Hulk*, *Fantastic Four*, and *Batman*. I was older now. Wouldn't be cool to get caught scanning the comic book racks.

But there was one I couldn't' give up. One I still clung to. One I was willing to sneak out and purchase, quickly and quietly, like a thief in the night.

Kid Colt.

I loved *Kid Colt* like a ten-year-old loves puppies. The Kid was cool. Only needed one gun. Had a horse named Steel, and a back story that'd make you cry. Well, maybe not *cry*. But, you know. The Kid lived by a creed (a Donovan Creed, you ask?) The Kid was an outlaw, wrongly accused. Went from town to town, always one step ahead of the law. Everywhere he went, he'd right a wrong.

Great stuff.

It's eight a.m. Saturday morning, my friends asleep. I enter the store, do a quick walk-through, pause briefly to see where my comic is situated on the display rack. Can't spend too much time at the rack, you know. Check the soft drinks, then the candy. I'd be less nervous buying condoms, tampons, a Playboy, or beer. Because those things a guy can laugh about with his buddies. Not comic books. Comic books are things that make your buddies laugh at *you*!

I rush to the display, grab my *Kid Colt*, set it on the counter with a dime and two pennies. No eye contact. Put the book in a bag and I'll be on my way. But no. Counter guy picks up my book. In a voice dripping with condescension, says, "Wow! *Kid Colt!* Fastest gun in the west! Fastest horse ever lived! And looky here," he says, pointing to the cover. "He's surrounded by a dozen men, guns blazing all around, but Kid Colt shoots them all!"

While he's saying all this, and more, I'm shrinking, mortified, horrified. He ends it with the dreaded, "Aren't you a little old for this stuff?" I stand there, saying nothing. He takes my coins, says, "Want a bag?" I nod, take it, and rush out the store.

I was crushed. He'd found my weakness, and made me suffer for it. My cheeks were on fire like Johnny Storm, *Fantastic Four*. Once home, I climbed on my bed, opened the cover of my beloved *Kid Colt*. Read a few words, stopped, stood, gathered all my comics, added this one to the pile, and lovingly placed them in the trash can.

I'd lost my innocence.

February, 2011.

That's when I published, against the advice of everyone I know, a western adventure titled *Follow the Stone*. People said "Westerns are dead. If you publish a Western, you'll lose the audience you've worked so hard to build." They said, "If you *must* write the damn thing, at least use a pen name!"

I wrote the book. Put my real name on it because...well, because I'm proud of it. You say you don't like Westerns? I hope to change your mind. I'm writing a series of John Locke Westerns, meaning, Westerns with a smirk. In doing so, I'm reclaiming a piece of my youth.

A few years back, my daughter's friends thought she was too old to like certain types of toys. So my wife and I took her into toy stores and pretended we were picking out toys for younger kids. "I'm sure she'd like this one!" our daughter would say, with bright, happy eyes. Years later, we did the same for our son. When their friends came over, we'd put these "kid toys" in a box. We kept their toy secret all that time, and I wouldn't tell you now, except that we're friends, you and me. I think you understand why I wanted my kids to enjoy their youthful indulgences as long as possible.

Which brings me to why I'm telling you all this: I want you to download my Western for only 99 cents, a friendship rate.

You know Donovan Creed, and I'm honored you like him. There's only one Creed, only one Callie. But the same author who brought Creed and Callie to the dance has lovingly crafted a whole new group of friends you need to meet. This ain't your grandpa's Western—it's totally cool and hip and funny. You're gonna love Emmett, Gentry, Shrug, and the rest of the gang.

I guarantee it.

Did I mention it's the #1 Western on Amazon/Kindle? Has been, for six weeks. But don't read it because it's popular. Read it because it's fun.

Give it a try. Find your childhood smile.

Here's the link. Click it now, before the world gets you sidetracked: *Follow the Stone*

While *Follow the Stone* was the #1 Western on Amazon/Kindle at the time, and had been for six weeks, it was about to fall out of the top 100. I wrote this blog, then did a Twitter search for comic books, childhood toys, westerns, and several other tags. I found people on Twitter who had hash-tagged some of these key words. Then I sent them a tweet with a link to my blog. I also announced the blog to my 20,000 Twitter followers, and many of my Twitter friends and pals re-tweeted it to *their* followers. The result? The book experienced renewed momentum. Sales increased to the point it made sense to write a sequel. So I did.

What About this *"How To"* Book?

This book has such an obvious market, it might appear there's no need to write a blog to attract readers. A simple announcement targeting authors would suffice, right?

Not necessarily.

A series of well-positioned announcements and author blogs would help me reach my exact target audience easily. But let's think a minute and see if we can create an additional market.

I can already hear you saying, "John: you, yourself said the only people interested in buying this book are authors and author hopefuls! What other market could possibly be out there?"

There is one other. Yes, authors are the only ones who would be interested in buying this *eBook*. But what about the paperback version? The eBook appeals to authors, but the paperback offers *additional* marketing opportunities, if I design my blog properly.

And what market is that?

The market of everyone who *knows* an author! Wouldn't my paperback book make a great Christmas gift for the author in your life?

If I decide to write such a blog, I would post it around Thanksgiving, in time for the Christmas season. My blog would need to get into the buyer's head and appeal to his or her emotions. How would I go about writing such a blog?

The first question I always ask, is *who is my audience, and what do they want?* I think I know. In fact, I'm so sure about it, I'll probably make this the blog title:

The Perfect Gift for Self-Published Authors!

The tags will be fantastic! By tagging it under Gifts, Christmas, Christmas Gifts, Top 10 Christmas Gifts, Authors, Self-Publishing, Books, etc. I will probably get linked to a number of blog lists that feature unique Christmas gift ideas. I could go on and on with the possibilities, but you get the point, right?

As for the actual message in the blog, I'll need a month to think it out and compose it, but in general...

I'll probably start with something personal, to show empathy. As a self-published author I know how hard it was to get people to read my books. I'll be talking to your loved ones about you, the author in their life.

I'll identify what you want (fame, a best-selling book, royalties...but more importantly, acceptance, and most of all, respect. Your loved ones are going to buy you a gift that shows they respect you and want you to achieve respect among your author peer group).

I'll explain why you want it, which will be the same reason I wanted it.

I'll explain how it does NOT make you feel. In other words, you're a good person. You're not angry, jealous or envious of successful authors. Then I'll explain how it DOES make you feel not to have it (hurt, frustrated, unfulfilled), and how it would make you feel if you DID have it (proud, self-satisfied, validated as an author).

I'll mention how others have asked me to help mentor them because of my success.

I'll tell them how I responded, and what I've done to solve your problem (meaning, I wrote this "How To" book).

I'll explain what the book will do for their author loved one.

I'll show them how easy it is to get my book under your Christmas tree (only $9.95 when you click this link!) so their loved one (you) can have the one thing you need to achieve spectacular success: (my system).

I'll admit to your loved ones that it's a shameless promotion, but I'll explain that my intentions are true. And because they really *are* true, your loved ones will know it.

Life-Changing Blogs:

I've been doing this for seven months now.

I've got a pretty good handle on how to do it, and how valuable these blogs can be. They're not easy to write, and you might not hit a home run the first few tries. It may turn out that you're not very good at writing them, or figuring out how to apply the concept to your books.

My answer to these problems is practice. Get feedback. Keep good records. Try harder!

I wish I had the time to teach a blog-writing seminar, and maybe I will at some point. But right now I have a full-time job. In addition, I typically spend several hours a day answering emails. I do interviews and guest blogs (when I have time), and spend a month hammering out the details of the blogs I personally write. I have a family with two kids who are active in sports and like being there for all their games. And somewhere in all those obligations of time, I'm an author who tries to write a novel every eight weeks!

I'm not overwhelmed, but I can *see* overwhelmed from here!

So I don't have time to help you write a blog. But if you take these tools and write a special blog you'd like me to read, I would *love* to have you send me a link! It doesn't have to be perfect; it just has to be something you're proud of! That's something I would make time to read, every time! Even if there are 10,000 of you who send me a link!

Now I'd like to close by talking about loyalty, and the OOU's.

Loyalty and the OOU's

I'VE GIVEN YOU what I've learned so far. It should be enough to help you earn far more than the price of this book. But I want to end with this:

As I said earlier, I want a deep following for my books, not a wide one. I'd rather have 100,000 rabid fans than a million luke-warm ones, or two million who try you once and move along. And there are ways to build loyalty.

My most loyal readers are the group I call OOU's. It means "One of Us." People want to be a part of something special and grand. They want to feel important, and want their opinions to count. If you're an OOU it means you've read all my books, and we've exchanged emails, and you know your opinion counts with me. It means I listen to you, and take your comments into consideration when I write my books. It means I appreciate you even more than you appreciate my books and characters. It means I care what happens to you in your life. It means I will always answer your emails. It means we're in this writing adventure together, as partners and friends, and I will work hard to always remain true to the characters and stories you have grown to love.

The loyal connection I have with my target audience is something I will never take for granted. The loyalty starts with me.

I write my books the way my target audience wants to read them. When I start to stray, they tell me, and I get back in line. If I want to try something different, I'll write a book outside my Donovan Creed and Emmett Love series.

I don't write by committee, but I constantly ask my OOU's for feedback. Most OOU's don't wait to be asked! If they love something, or hate it, I hear about it in no uncertain terms!

I keep my books as affordable as possible for my loyal readers. I call it my "friendship price," and if the day comes when I increase my prices, I'll give my OOU's two or three weeks advance notice, so they can always pay the lowest possible price.

I always respond to my readers' emails. I don't believe my time is more valuable than theirs. I'm honored they want to check in with me, and although sometimes I don't answer immediately, they know I'll answer as soon as I can.

I love my OOU's and they know it. If you go to my website, www.DonovanCreed.com, you will see a store that offers OOU T-shirts! I didn't create this store to take advantage of my OOU's. I didn't even *want* a store! But my OOU's demanded the T-shirts!

My OOU's show their loyalty by writing reviews, blogging, tweeting, and spreading the word about my books to their friends and relatives. It truly is a partnership, and one that's based on the sense of humor we share, and the fun I have writing to them, and the fun they have reading my silly stuff. In the final analysis, even though I take a business approach to writing, publishing, and marketing my books, that's what it's all about for my readers and me: **FUN**.

Thank You!

THANK YOU FOR buying and reading this book and trusting me to offer something of value. I sincerely hope you use these concepts to eclipse every milestone I've achieved!

Although I've repeatedly whined about being so busy, I'd be thrilled to hear from you about your experiences. You know the drill! Go to my website and click on the "Contact" button! That's how our friendship will start, if we're not already great friends!

I hope you'll consider subscribing to my blog at www.DonovanCreed.com

If you go there you'll see two posts I've written specifically for authors. One is *Break Some Rules!* The other is titled, *Bad Reviews!* These blogs weren't written to sell a specific product, but rather to offer advice to my author friends. Now that you know how I think, and how I approach blogging, and know what to look for in my future blogs...

It would be a huge honor if you decide to subscribe! That would prove this book had a positive impact on you! Naturally, I'd also love for you to buy one of my books and save it for a day you need a few extra smiles. But even if you choose not to, we can still be friends, yes?

Best wishes, always!

John

John Locke

The New York Times Best Selling Author
#1 Best Selling Author on Amazon Kindle

Donovan Creed Series:

Lethal People
Lethal Experiment
Saving Rachel
Now & Then
Wish List
A Girl Like You
Vegas Moon

Emmett Love Series:

Follow the Stone
Don't Poke the Bear!

To contact John Locke, or to be placed on a mailing list to receive updates about new releases, click the "Contact Me" tab on his website: http://www.DonovanCreed.com

CPSIA information can be obtained at www.ICGtesting.com
Printed in the USA
238235LV00001B/399/P

9 781935 670919